THE REBIRTH OF HOPE

MY JOURNEY
FROM VIETNAM WAR CHILD
TO AMERICAN CITIZEN

SAU LE HUDECEK

Fort Worth, Texas

Library of Congress Cataloging-in-Publication Data

Names: Hudecek, Sau Le, author.
Title: The rebirth of hope : my journey from Vietnam War child to American
citizen / Sau Le Hudecek.
Description: Fort Worth, Texas : TCU Press, [2017]
Identifiers: LCCN 2016045098 (print) | LCCN 2016046296 (ebook) |
ISBN 9780875654324 (alk. paper) | ISBN 9780875656625
Subjects: LCSH: Hudecek, Sau Le. | Vietnamese American women--
Texas--Fort Worth--Biography. | Vietnamese Americans--Texas--Fort Worth--
Biography. | Racially mixed people--Texas--Fort Worth--Biography. | Women
    immigrants--Texas--Fort Worth--Biography. | Immigrants--Texas--Fort
    Worth--Biography. | Beauty operators--Texas--Fort Worth--Biography. |
    Hudecek, Sau Le--Childhood and youth. | Vietnam War, 1961-1975--Children.
    | Vietnamese Americans--Cultural assimilation--Texas--Fort Worth.
Classification: LCC E184.V53 H83 2017 (print) | LCC E184.V53 (ebook) | DDC
    305.48/895922073--dc23
LC record available at https://lccn.loc.gov/2016045098

TCU Press
TCU Box 298300
Fort Worth, Texas 76129
817.257.7822
www.prs.tcu.edu
To order books: 1.800.826.8911

Designed by Bill Brammer
www.fusion29.com

In order to protect their privacy, the names of some of the individuals in this book have
been changed.

Through God
To our country
For my family
This is my testimony

Contents

Acknowledgments

In many ways completing this book has mirrored my life. It has been a long journey where I learned a lot and received help from many people along the way.

First, I would like to thank June Naylor Harris, who spent many hours listening to me and taking notes so that she could get down on paper the initial facts of my story, which allowed me to finally move forward with this dream of mine that sat dormant for many years.

Once I had the basic facts of my life captured, Don read my story and said that now we needed to turn the facts of my life into the story of my life. We needed help. I searched the Internet for a local editor who could help me, and when I read the profile of Leslie Lutz, I just knew she was the one. She provided Don and me guidance for organizing my story by themes instead of a chronological start-here-and-end-there structure. She also taught me how to show and tell my story, where I had so far only listed important facts. For almost a year she worked with Don and me as we added to my story piece by piece, using her outline as our roadmap. Leslie was a Godsend if there ever was one.

I want to thank my husband Don, who acted as a liaison between Leslie and me. He would coax me along when she suggested that I dig into various parts of my life in order to mine the detail needed to flesh out my story. This was not always easy for him or me, especially for certain episodes that were attached to painful memories, but since he knew this book was important to me, he held my feet to the fire even though he was also getting burned in the process. I believe that we came out the other side even stronger for it.

I would also like to thank my mom, Uyen Hoang. In addition to long ago making the decision to give birth to me when she knew the hardships that would follow, she spent many phone calls with me rehashing old and buried memories from her youth up to my early childhood. I know reliving these memories was often difficult for her, and in addition to providing critical detail for my story, those conversations also provided me long-sought insight into how I came to be.

Once I had the first solid draft of my book completed, I needed to consider how I would publish it. One day at my salon, my friend Dee Dee mentioned to one of her customers, Jean Roach, that I had written a book. Jean thought that was exciting and asked what it was about. When I told her about the book, she asked if she could read it. She also mentioned that TCU had a really good publishing house and that I should reach out to them. When I mentioned that I wouldn't know who to reach out to or how and asked for her help, she gladly said yes. After reading the book she sent it on to TCU Press on my behalf. She was another in the chain of angels in my life.

Working with everyone at TCU Press has been a joy, even though at times I am sure my nature to negotiate everything as if I were at a Vietnamese market tested their patience. Their understanding and true concern for my well-being touched me greatly, and I know in my heart I was supposed to be with them on this journey.

I also want to acknowledge two groups that made it possible for me to come to America and jump-start my life here: Travis Avenue Baptist Church, my sponsor, and World Relief. Both helped me through my initial transition into this society.

Finally, I want to acknowledge my friends and customers who throughout the years have mentored me in the English language and American culture, and who have always been there when I needed support. It's through their kindness that I have become part of our American family.

One

When I was six years old, the night before school started, my sister was killed by a land mine.

I was watching a movie when it happened. That always seems to be the case when something terrible arrives on your doorstep, that you are watching a movie, or washing the dishes, or buying something at the market. And then comes the knock at the door—or in my case, the announcement over the theater's PA system—that tells you the ordinary is gone, and you have horror in its place.

I had been playing with a friend at an outdoor theater in Quảng Tri, the small town where I grew up in Vietnam. A voice blared over the speakers, but it was muddled by the noise and the crowd's reaction to the news. Confused, I followed everyone as they left the theater and ran toward the scene, and as I was running with them, I started to pick out pieces of what had happened. As I did, a sense of dread built in me, fueled by the panic that lit the faces in the crowd. Three people had stepped on a land mine. One person was dead, they were sure, and they couldn't find two others. It was getting dark, and they needed everyone to help look for them. The crowd hummed with pieces of facts, rumor, and confusion.

At this point I had not seen my sister Tho for a while. Everyone was talking about death, and I wasn't really sure what they were talking about. I don't remember who took me home, but I got home somehow and went to bed, still believing my sister would come home to me.

The next day they found Tho very far away from the explosion, her body miraculously intact. She had died from the impact—the bones of her small body shattered by hitting the ground so hard. When my mother saw her, carried limp on the shoulder of a family friend, she collapsed. Her darling Tho, taken away so young, and by a fragment of a war that was supposed to be over. But during the traditional three-day funeral, even though the mourners had plenty of opportunity to comment bitterly on the unfairness of it all, none of the hundreds of people that came to give their respects to the wood box in the center of our living room mentioned

1

anything about the war. It was considered a sign of respect to my sister to keep those comments to themselves.

It is hard to explain how people felt about the land mines, even in the context of a tragedy like ours. The mines were placed by both sides, but people felt that the bulk of them were buried by Americans. Most South Vietnamese thought fighting the Viet Cong was the right thing to do, so they didn't want to blame their American allies. The occasional senseless death, even that of a child, was part of the cost of fighting for what you felt was right. At least that was the opinion of many of my neighbors. The Viet Cong, on the other hand, didn't want to do or say anything that made their "victory" seem any less glorious. When someone lost a family member, the South Vietnamese would blame the war (you could not blame the Viet Cong openly), and the Viet Cong would blame the Americans, and the blame would be passed around. This lashing out was usually just a momentary thing, an outgrowth of their grief, and was usually said behind closed doors. In Vietnam in the 1970s, you always had to be conscious of what you said.

At the age of six, I didn't know anything about land mines. All I could see was my mother crying and passing out from time to time, my brother weeping as I had never seen him do before, and this strange wood box in the middle of the house. I did not know I was in the presence of death. I wondered, what is this wood box that wasn't in our house before?

I stopped asking questions about the box since nobody answered them. Finally, my brother came up to me, grabbed my shoulders, and said that my sister had died. But you might as well have told me the sun wouldn't rise in the morning. I asked him what he meant.

"Do you understand that she is gone and never coming back?" he asked me, his eyes unusually gentle.

"What do you mean that she is never coming back? Where did she go?"

Eventually someone told me that my sister was in the box, but I couldn't see her. I later learned that my family built the coffin, as is our custom in Vietnam. Since embalming wasn't a part of our rituals, my family dressed her body in white and filled the coffin with dirt. Then her coffin was sealed and tied up tightly so that no one could smell the inevitable decay. Perhaps it is gruesome, but it is the way all of us in Vietnam pass from the world of the living to the dead.

I walked around the house during those three days seeing so many people coming and going, I wondered, *what is death*? I asked people what it was, and the hours blurred into something crazy and fuzzy and strange. I wasn't crying, just confused as I tried to figure out what happened. I remember my brother crying—something he so rarely did—and so many people at my house weeping and still talking about death.

Three days later, when they took the box and buried it, I was still confused. I asked my mom, "How will my sister be able to get out of the box with all of the dirt on it? Will she get cold? Will she get wet when it rains?" I still didn't know why my sister would go in the box and not come back. I sat on the pile of dirt watching the incense sticks burn, wondering why my family and the whole town were crying.

* * * *

After the funeral, I learned that the whole town loved Tho because she was smart, beautiful, and very sweet and kind to everyone. She always put everyone else above herself.

Not long before her death, my sister was invited to visit Ho Chi Minh's grave, an honor which is usually reserved for people in the Viet Cong. This was strange in many ways since not only were we not Viet Cong, but our family fought on the side of the Americans. Even stranger, my sister was related to me—a mixed Vietnamese and American child. She was invited because she had high achievements in school and because she had very beautiful writing. I remember seeing one of her letters or an article or something that was packaged in plastic to preserve it. I guess that her achievements, whatever they may have been, were big enough to override the normal prejudice that stained a family such as ours.

* * * *

People often said that Tho was the perfect child. Several people were cruel enough to ask me, "Why did she die when you are still here?" At the time, I still didn't really understand what her dying meant, but the comments didn't really hurt too much. Abuse was normal for me. I was blamed for everything, no matter the cause. I was the "bad child," the child who shamed everyone. I had never really taken the blaming to heart because it was so frequent, and often so crazy, that it didn't make sense.

I remember one night, before Tho died, when we were eating dinner outside, and the wind whipped up and blew out the wick of the diesel lamp on the table. It was our only light, and everyone started yelling at me, "Why did you blow out the light?!" My mom even whipped me, probably to calm everyone down. Tho stood up for me and said that it wasn't my fault, and that they should not blame me.

Although this constant conditioning thickened my skin against the blaming, I remember it. My older sister, Huong, had friends who were Viet Cong, and she wanted to be Viet Cong to make her life easier, but she couldn't because of me. My older sister didn't say these things to me, only to other people. In fact, my older sister never really talked to me at all, good or bad—I just really wasn't in the picture for her. She seemed to put blame for my half-American, half-Vietnamese existence on my mom, not on me like the others did.

3

My brother Huy Van didn't seem to be able to cope with how his life was impacted by my existence. Often when his friends saw me on the street and made fun of me, he came home and beat me. "Don't go out on the street again!" he would say.

Of course, this was impossible. I had to go out on errands to buy food and laundry powder. If I didn't completely finish the cooking or the laundry in time, someone would beat me for that, too. Every culture has an expression for this situation that we call a catch-22 here in America.

From the time I was six years old, there wasn't much that I could do to avoid my brother's fist. That was the year my mother told me I was old enough to wash everyone's clothes. No one taught me how, so I had to figure it out the best that I could. My brother had a pair of white jeans and we had a red dirt floor. My first day on laundry duty, I did my best. I carried the laundry to the river where piece by piece I dipped the clothing in the water and rubbed the fabric together using the laundry powder, which was more like sand than soap and didn't foam up. I had to spend about five times as long on my brother's jeans to get the red dirt out. Afterwards I carried the laundry home, which was harder than the trip to the river since the clothes were now wet. When I got back I hung the clothes over a wire to dry, flipping them over the top of the wire trying to balance the sides evenly since we didn't have clothespins to prevent the clothes from falling off the wire. When the clothes were dry I needed to get the wrinkles out. I heated a heavy skillet in the fire pit and then placed the iron on it to heat up. The iron was made of cast iron with a thin, smooth layer of copper on the bottom and had a handle that got hot, so I had to hold it with a towel. When I finished ironing I put everyone's clothes on hangers and hung them on the nails on the bed posts where we hung our mosquito nets. I finally finished and then had to work on the cooking.

Later, when my brother came home, he turned the jeans inside out. And there it was. A red spot inside the hem. From his reaction, you would have thought I had ripped the jeans in half and thrown trash on them. But ultimately, his rage wasn't about the jeans. It was about being related to me.

For these kinds of failures Huy Van used his fists as a lesson. If he was feeling creative, he beat me with a big branch. For special occasions, he might even throw a chair at me. But no matter how I got the bruises, the end result was me washing everything again. If the stain was stubborn, he beat me again. I remember sitting in the corner of the house with tears streaming down my face, my arms and legs still throbbing from the blows, wishing I could tell him to wash his own clothes. And good luck with those stupid white jeans. But I was so scared. A complaint would only bring more beatings.

I noticed a small wasp nest above his bed and thought that if I could loosen the nest just enough, then it might fall on top of him while he was sleeping. I didn't think of what would actually cause the nest to fall at just the right time, but this image of my brother getting stung, screaming in pain, gave me great satisfaction, so I decided to make it happen. I got a knife and climbed on my brother's bed. I still couldn't reach the nest, so I found a long stick and tied the knife to the end of it. Now I could reach the nest from the floor, which I thought would be safer. I got to work on the small stem that attached the nest to the ceiling, which was flimsy but a lot harder to cut than I had expected. During the entire time I was imagining how this scene would play out and anticipating the great satisfaction I would experience by getting revenge. Never once did I consider the realities of trying to make it happen. Since I was focused on slicing the nest's flimsy stem until it was just thin enough, I didn't pay any mind to the nest swinging to and fro. Two small wasps flew out of the nest, and one stung me on my index finger. How can something so small cause so much pain?

Lying on the floor squeezing my finger, eventually my head cleared enough that I realized how stupid I had been. At first I felt cheated by being robbed of my chance for revenge, but then I remembered about karma. Based on what I had been told, I had always thought it would be balanced over my entire life, but it seems a single evil act has the power to sting me back no matter how justified I may feel about committing it. The pain ensured that this was a lesson I would remember for a long time. But the learning and even the ache soon gave way to worry as I thought about how to delay the next beating for as long as possible.

Just when I thought I might break from too much abuse, my sister Tho would come home. It was like having an angel in the room. She would stop him, and those were the best moments of my childhood, when she was there to protect me. But then she was out again, working, and no one else, not even my mom, would try to stop my brother's wrath. Looking back, God must have been watching out for me. Otherwise, I would surely have been killed by one of these beatings.

My sister Tho was the only person who never treated me as something to blame. Then one day she was gone, and she was never coming back. The day I lost my sister, I lost the one voice that would always speak out for me and protect me. This is why I believed that when my sister died, I lost my lifeline to hope.

Two

My mother lived in the demilitarized zone (DMZ), close to the American side, so when she was widowed with three children, she got a job with the American camps doing laundry for American soldiers. Then I happened.

Six years later, a man told me the government would take me away from my family, along with all of the other American children, and put a bullet in my head.

The day I learned I would die was like any other day. I was at my sister's shop, which consisted of a small tailor business and an adjacent café, a common setup in Vietnam. On this particular afternoon, I sat off to one corner, minding Huong's tiny boy and girl, when an unassuming man came in to get something to eat. My sister fetched his bowl of noodles and went back to her work. Bending over her sewing machine as he ate, she made polite conversation.

As the stranger ate his lunch, he talked about himself. He was a prisoner on his way to jail, imprisoned for helping the Americans during the war. Looking back now, I realize it must seem odd to Americans—prisoners wandering about free, ordering lunch in shops. But in Vietnam, when prisoners were transferred from one jail to another, they weren't moved by car or bus. The jailor told them where to go and walked them there, and if they wanted to get a bite to eat on the way, why not? No one would be crazy enough to attempt an escape, not in Vietnam. It wasn't a free country, and it wasn't a place where you could just blend in, since in most communities everyone knew everyone else. There was nowhere for you to run.

I definitely didn't blend in. The prisoner finally noticed me with the toddlers in the corner.

"See this little girl?" He pointed at me. "This American?" He spat the word. "The government will come here and shoot her."

He might as well have shot me himself. A hot pain tore through my heart. The panic exploded inside me, knocking the breath out of me, as my thoughts raced: *Will they warn me first? Will I have one eye open when they shoot me, or will they give me time to close my eyes?*

Standing there next to my sister, I watched this man's face for a hint of a lie, or insanity, something that would tell me it wasn't true. My sister had been concentrating on her work, focusing on the dress seam she was sewing, with her brows knitted together. But when he spoke, she raised her head and turned her face to him, her expression changing from focus on her work to complete confusion and surprise.

Then she did something she had never done for me before. She stood up for me.

"Why would anyone shoot her? She didn't do anything. Wouldn't they come after her mother instead?"

Tho, now gone, was the one who would always defend me, but never Huong. In fact, Huong never before even acknowledged my situation. She mostly acted as if I did not exist. But here she was, defending me. My sister and I never discuss that day. It would be years before I would understand how hard her life was made by having me as her little sister.

Though she defended me, I didn't feel better. All I could think was: *If someone does come after my mother, what will happen to me?*

But I would not speak to my mother about it. To bring up this terrifying incident and my burning fear would only deepen her grief, and even as a small girl, I understood that. The person who could have truly comforted me was my dead sister. Even Huong putting her words in front of me like a shield was not enough to soften the blow.

The man finished his lunch and left, continuing his walk to his new prison. He probably didn't think about me again, probably didn't know he laid the thread of something terrible in my brain, something that had only been made of shadow before. I became a child always waiting for someone to make good on the prisoner's promise. That day marked the beginning of fear for me, and I carry the shadow of that feeling with me even now, as I write this memoir. Like the prisoner, I had nowhere to run.

* * * *

I was one of three children fathered by Americans in my hometown of Quảng Tri, but I was the only one whose father was a black American. My dark skin and curly hair were shocking to everyone where I lived. Even as a little girl I was a freak, and every day, countless people noticed me and asked my family in veiled terms how I would survive. Frozen, I never expected anything good to happen to me. Hopes? Dreams? Beyond my reach. I had no right to expect to ever be in love, to have a happy life—nothing. I wonder sometimes if my mother ever felt as I did, as if she had nowhere to run—caught in a war she didn't cause, caught by a love she didn't expect, pregnant with a child who would forever mark her as a traitor to the Viet Cong. Only *one* of those realities is enough to break someone, but she survived.

Unless you look back a century or so, it's hard for anyone outside of Vietnamese culture to comprehend the utter disgrace of the crime against decency she committed by getting pregnant out of wedlock. In Vietnamese culture, you must be a virgin when you get married. Even if you are a widow and no longer a virgin, sex outside of marriage was nothing less than eternal shame. My mother was a single widow who had a child out of wedlock. This was a sin. That she chose one who was now considered "the enemy" as her partner in sin only made her more incomprehensible to her family and her community.

She was an outcast, and I, fathered by an American soldier, was an abomination. Nobody asked who my father was. It didn't matter. And when she was giving birth to me, her own sisters wouldn't come help, as is the custom in Vietnam. They wouldn't come see her new baby. I try to imagine what it was like for her, alone in the birthing room, every contraction reminding her of what she had lost. When you are poor, all you have is your pride and reputation. When you lose that, you have nothing. How much strength does it take to keep going in the face of such loss?

* * * *

My mother, Uyen Thi Hoang, was born in Quảng Tri. When Vietnam was divided into North and South in the 1950s, Quảng Tri became the most northern province in the Republic of Vietnam, and American bases were established there in the 1960s. My mother's home—which would one day become my birthplace—was some seven hundred miles from Saigon, now called Ho Chi Minh City. The landscape is richly green and quite beautiful in many ways, surrounded by the scenic Annamite Mountains, which have high slopes over seven thousand feet with rugged tops and narrow valleys. The land is fertile, and forest covers much of the region.

My mother became a farm worker at fourteen and was married at eighteen. She started a successful stall in a market where she served food and sold spices and various foodstuffs. She and her husband had four children, of which three survived. In 1966 her husband died in the Vietnam War fighting alongside the Americans. She found herself a widow at thirty-one.

Her business immediately ran into trouble. People who once kept their word to her husband didn't feel the same obligation to his widow. They refused to pay back loans and failed to make good on verbal promises after they had taken items from her stall. She had to shut down her shop. Soon after, as the fighting made its way to Quảng Tri, the government relocated her and her family to another town about an hour away.

What was life like for my mother then? I cannot truly grasp it. I can only guess at the difficulty she endured as a young widow with three children to feed in a terrifying time in our country's history.

During the worst of the fighting in Quảng Trị, both before and after her relocation, my mother and her stepmother did all they could to protect the children from stray bombs and bullets. During the day they would often hide with the children in tunnels as both sides dropped bomb after bomb, shaking the earth, each explosion threatening to bury them alive. During the night, when the fighting usually stopped or slowed down, my mother and her stepmom would go out in what was left of the fields, after the fighting and the bombs tore them up, to collect water and gather rice and vegetables for the family. Eventually the land was upside down to the point that it was almost impossible to harvest anything. I imagine what she looked like, bending over in the fields looking for grains of rice and finding shrapnel instead. Her body became a machine, her hands desperate sifters, and for those hours, her sole purpose was to pick through the violent remains of war, hoping to find something that still had life in it.

Although I can't really know what it was like, I do know this—my mother was a strong woman. She didn't collapse under the weight of war and loneliness. She was the lifeblood of the family, the provider, the one who sweat to bring home whatever she could to ensure her family's survival.

In the spring of 1967, when the American soldiers in our country numbered over four hundred thousand, my mother found a job filling sandbags for the US military. After a while, her employers began to trust her and gave her what was considered a good job washing clothes at the offices of American military personnel in Quảng Trị. Our people took the jobs they could find, and it wasn't entirely unusual for someone like Mom to find the job she did.

For the first two years, my mother worked for the US Marines as a housekeeper hired by a group of Vietnamese who both provided Vietnamese helpers for Americans and translated for them. These jobs were highly sought after because of the pay as well as the prestige. When the Americans discovered that my mom had a cousin who was Viet Cong, she was fired. I can envision her panic when she received the note, its crisp bureaucratic language telling her she was no longer welcome. If she had left them, head bowed, defeated, she would have never met my father, and I wouldn't have existed. But corruption had taken hold of the American bases in our region, and she easily bought her way back into a job by bribing the Vietnamese handlers who worked with the marines. She had worked for the army for only a month when she met my father, an officer overseeing people in the motor pool. My father's driver would pick up the four ladies at 8:00 a.m. to wash clothes for the group that my mom knew as unit number fourteen, and then he would take them home at 4:30 p.m. My father's job didn't take him into combat, so he was around the camp during the day when she was working.

Even though the thirty-five thousand Dong a month that the Vietnamese handlers paid my mother to wash clothes was good pay for someone of my mom's status, she soon found a way to make extra money on the side to better support her family. The soldiers wanted to look good when they went to the club and didn't feel like shining their shoes after spending the day out on patrol. My mom offered to shine the shoes of one soldier who was impressed with her work. He told others. Through word of mouth, my mom soon was shining on average five pairs of shoes a month. That may not sound like much, but it brought in an extra four thousand Dong a month, which meant a lot to the typical Vietnamese family. Because of her very limited English, my mom would use her fingers to show how much she would charge for a given task—which earned her the nickname "Fingers."

Since American goods were highly sought after by the wealthy Vietnamese, instead of money, my mom asked to be paid in cigarettes that the soldiers could buy in the commissary—two packs for each pair of shoes. She then sold them for eight hundred Dong per pack to people who owned stalls in the local market. Once people found out she had American cigarettes for sale, they were waiting at the end of the day for her and the other three women who worked at the base, milling about the spot just outside the base where the jeep would drop them off, all of them hoping to be the first ones to buy whatever my mom had.

Getting the cigarettes off base was tricky since she could lose her job, so she packed the cigarettes in a butter container that she stashed under the seat of the Jeep. The MPs always searched my mother and the other women when they entered and left the base, but they never searched the American driver or his vehicle. She never told my father that she was smuggling the goods off the base to add to the money she made washing clothes, so my father had no idea that my mother was using her military driver as a cigarette mule.

Even though my mother's English was limited, she and my father began to communicate. I can picture what it was like, my father offering to drive the women even though it was someone else's job, her hidden stash of cigarettes under her seat, the whine and roar of the engine making his unfamiliar words even harder to understand as he tried to flirt. Perhaps she read more in his eyes than she did in his words. Perhaps there was something in his laugh that made their communication pure and perfect. Perhaps the war tearing up the world around them made them feel how precious those stolen moments were. In any case, she fell in love with him, and he with her.

Being very proper and proud, my mother was not someone who would have a meaningless relationship, but they could never be together in any family sense—they had no choice but to keep their love a guarded secret. My mother lived in the shadow of the Viet Cong, and their hatred of the Americans and the Vietnamese soldiers who fought with them was violent and powerful. Although they tolerated the Vietnamese who worked on an American base—after all, they understood the nature of poverty and desperation—her *personal* association with anyone in the American military was unthinkable. People related to soldiers who fought with the South Vietnamese alongside the Americans lived in fear. The kind of association my mother had with my father wasn't just forbidden by culture and prejudice—it was dangerous. And I assume that for him, it was equally out of the question for his relationship with my mother to be known.

After my father and mother had known each other for about two years, she became pregnant with me. Then my father left Vietnam. And so, like my sisters and my brother, I grew up without a father.

The details of my mother's life—her struggles, her dreams, her mistakes—were hidden inside her for a very long time. In fact, I didn't hear most of my mother's story until we had resettled in America. She still becomes suspicious of me when I ask her questions about the past.

Why did my mother never tell me her story before? When I was younger, I saw her cry now and then. I asked her once why she was crying, and she said her sister wouldn't visit her, that her old friends had stopped speaking to her. Sometimes in the middle of her tears she would say she was sorry, but my attempts to make this conversation go further never really went anywhere. It hurt, but all I could do was to accept that my mother was a closed book.

As time went on, I somehow came to understand that she wouldn't talk to me about her feelings because to live through the nightmare of war and the loss of her honor was anguish enough. Translating her emotions into language, discussing them with someone—even me—was nothing less than torture for her. As I grew up, I figured out that forcing a conversation only made her more miserable. She was carrying a terrible burden as it was.

After I was born, the government relocated my mother, along with many others, to an area near Hanoi. She had to walk the entire distance, holding a five-month-old baby and whatever possessions she could carry. It was cold in Hanoi, but she was afraid to bring the only warm blanket she had because "USA" was emblazoned across it.

When she finally returned years later to her house in Quảng Tri, all of her possessions were gone. Sometimes she would see her things in other people's houses, but she never asked for them back. She had abandoned her home, and she had no proof that those things were ever hers. And if she wanted to raise any ruckus about the theft, she would have to stand in front of government officials—all of whom were Viet Cong—with a half-American baby in her arms.

After we returned to Quảng Tri to our empty house, a friend told us that my father had knocked on her door, looking for my mother. He had asked for directions to our home and had come to find her, but she wasn't home. No one knew our location, and our neighbor told him that my mom was pregnant, but she wasn't sure her English was good enough to make him understand. He couldn't stay long, he told our neighbor. He didn't have the time to search the country, so he left without her.

What did he feel that day leaving Quảng Tri with nothing, after flying back over the ocean to find the woman he'd left behind? But his trip was not entirely futile. Although I could never talk to my mother about her feelings, I can imagine that it eased her heart to know that he loved her enough to come back.

Of course, she never talked about him, his romantic attempt to find her, or how she felt about the father of her child—not with the ears of the Viet Cong around every corner. She was terrified of the Viet Cong, although none of them actively came after her—she had cousins high up in their ranks. As long as she kept a low profile, she would avoid punishment. She gave up any dreams of being an entrepreneur again—success would draw undue attention to her and me.

* * * *

Compounding the disgrace and complete rejection of my mother and our family was the fear that covered everyone in our town like a thick blanket. The communist government was a suffocating presence that kept the people in our region from knowing any real joy.

By 1967, the North Vietnamese began moving deeper into our region, and our city was occupied by the communist military. The Viet Cong were very strong in Quảng Tri; three years before I was born, a major battle in the Tet Offensive was fought there. Occupation of the area went back and forth between the North and the South, and the North Vietnamese captured my city again when I was a year old. The whole province came under North Vietnamese rule when I was four years old, making it an actively dangerous place for our family. We lived in great fear all the time, for many years.

The communist government was a terrifying force. They were proud of fighting and winning the war, and they often spoke loudly of their intelligence and superiority. Anything American was truly despised, and the American people were huge failures. The members of the communist government worshipped Ho Chi Minh deeply. In their eyes, nothing could compare to His Excellency.

The government was 100 percent Viet Cong. My mom was always afraid of what the government might do to me, her, and her other children. Those in charge told everyone what to do and had zero tolerance for not following orders. Men quit school at the age of eighteen to join the army; the government made exceptions only for families that had only one son. All men cut their hair short. Each person was taught a trade so he or she would become self-sufficient—communist officials had no interest in feeding anyone. The government would take their share of each crop without asking.

I found living under communist control to be more curse than anything else, although ignorance about our situation had an unexpected silver lining. On the one hand, since the Communists were all about making sure we had no clue what was happening anywhere else, we weren't free. On the other hand, not knowing was a kind of blessing. Since the government controlled news and communications, we weren't exposed to the constant negative flow of the news we have in the United States. Our lives became more bearable, and that constant ache that Americans have—always wanting this, always wanting that—just wasn't there for us. There was no media goading, and we didn't complain about how bad the economy was, what the Joneses had that we didn't, how limited our rights were, or how corrupt our government officials were. We only thought about the government when it directly impacted our lives. We focused on the business of living. We focused on survival. Living inside this paradox, I learned to count my blessings, no matter the circumstances.

Not having, as well as *not knowing*, was a kind of blessing as well. We didn't have "things" to occupy our time, so our primary source of entertainment was each other. Our community had an open door policy: if you wanted to visit someone, you walked to their house. If they were busy they would let you know, and your arrival was not taken as an intrusion of their space. No need to worry if it was an appropriate time. No need to worry that you would be wasting their time, or yours. Life wasn't run by the clock. You did what you needed to survive and to meet the level of comfort you desired.

This comfort wasn't about things, about *having*. Everyone knew everyone else and what people had in their homes—or, more appropriately, how little they had in their homes—so they had no fear of someone taking something. But more importantly, if community kinship and peer pressure wasn't enough to stop someone from breaking the rules, there was always the knowledge that there would be swift and stern punishment from the government. If you needed a teaspoon of salt, however, and your neighbor wasn't home, it was acceptable to take it, as people trusted that you would pay them back.

My mother hadn't stolen from our neighbors, and she hadn't sold government secrets to the enemy, but she was punished nonetheless. Strangely, that punishment wasn't overt—it was a subtle kind of neglect.

Family history is like a credit card. If your family had a good record—you fought for Viet Cong, etc.—you would be put first in line to get a good job or go to college. Smarts and skills were not considered if you didn't also have a good family history. Because I was a child of an American soldier, my family had no credit at all.

This bankrupt family history was front and center in everything we did.

The Communist government was a force that had a hand in almost every aspect of life, so it wasn't even worth it for us to try to better our family—the answer would always be no. Spots for anything worth having were always filled first by those with the right family credit card. Because our family history was bankrupt, we were always last in line. Since there was no one standing in line behind us, we were happy when we even got table scraps. It became harder and harder to see life in Vietnam as a blessing to be counted.

Three

Life in my old country was as totally different from life in America as you can imagine. Of course, I didn't know that at the time, because I had no way of knowing what life was like anywhere else. Even today, if people in Vietnam are lucky enough to have refrigerators, they might not be able to afford the electricity to run them. Refrigerators are used mainly to keep flies off of the food. Most Americans can't imagine the kind of existence that doesn't allow for the luxury of cold beverages and the convenience of fresh food that actually stays fresh for a week or more.

My childhood was totally Third World: No television. No telephones in the home. No electricity or running water in the home. Nothing modern about it. If we wanted water, we went to a well or the river. With no electricity, at night we read or did our work by a diesel lamplight or by candlelight. We cooked on a wood-burning stove.

We knew people whose home had no roof. We were fortunate that our house had a metal roof, along with metal walls, material we had scavenged from a landing field with some Quonset huts nearby. We had a central room and two bedrooms, and our floor was made of dirt. In our country, the parents slept in one bed and all the kids in another bed.

Our meals were very basic: rice and vegetables, and unlike the truly poor, we could periodically buy meat and fish if we had extra vegetables or chickens to sell. Meat was mostly for special occasions. Typically, we went to what could be called a supermarket every other week to buy staples such as salt. Since we had chickens, we didn't need to buy eggs. Almost everything was fresh; we cooked and ate everything the same day we bought it at the market. Other than rice, we had no foods with a shelf life because nothing had any preservatives. I always laugh when I hear what a big deal is made about natural or organic foods here, because that's all we had. What's interesting is that at least while I still lived in Vietnam, there seemed to be a very low incidence of cancer or illness there, and I think it's because the food is so simple.

I got a new set of clothing—I'm talking about one shirt and one pair of pants—once a year. We didn't go to the store to buy clothes; you went to the store to buy the cloth to make the clothes. Even though our clothes weren't expensively crafted or made with expensive fabric, they were tailor made for us and custom fitted. When you have one set of clothing, you take really good care of it. We would never wear dirty clothes; if we had to, we washed them every night so that we had clean clothes to wear the next day.

Over there, most never felt sorry or sad about material things we didn't have. We didn't take vacations. We didn't celebrate birthdays with special food or presents. We only celebrated the naming of a child one month after he or she was born, and then life went on from there. But I never saw anyone sit around being miserable about a lack of vacations or fancy food or birthday parties—because growing up the way I did, we didn't know any different. And we weren't even poor, really. We were not rich, but we had more than some people we knew, thanks to my mother's hard work.

We had no electronics to speak of, although we knew some people who had a radio. For recreation, we went swimming in the nearby rivers. There were no swimming pools or swimming lessons, ever. If you wanted to learn how to swim—and we all did—you just figured it out. Occasionally we would go to a movie. Neighbors just enjoyed spending time together, simply visiting with each other.

Although my personal experiences were inconsistent, the level of connectedness in our community was really quite astounding, especially from the perspective I have now. If someone wasn't home when we stopped by for a visit, we would either wait on their porch or let ourselves in and sit in their home until they returned. Usually, they were happy to have the company, and if they were busy, they were always polite. People greeted us and took time for a brief visit before letting us know that they were in a hurry to do something. They might say that they would be back by a certain time and that we were free to wait. If it wasn't going to be too long, we would wait in their home while they went about their errand or chore. If they had something to get done, we would often help them if we were able.

It was a blessing in a way that we didn't know what we didn't have. Except for me and others like me, there was no place for envy or feeling "less than." For most people, their family and neighbors were all they needed to make their lives feel whole.

Even though the closeness of our community is something I miss about my life in Vietnam, there are other aspects of village life I was happy to leave behind. It's hard for Americans to imagine what it is like to be completely at the mercy of the environment. Even the poorest here can find a clean drink of water on a moment's notice, but in my village, safe water was never a guarantee. The closest community well was about a half mile away from our house, but when we had dry seasons, this well would dry up. The whole town would then walk about four miles to the next well.

I often had to head out at 1:00 a.m. to get ahead of hundreds of people coming from other towns who also had lost their water source. The well could *almost* keep up with the number of people, but even in the middle of the night, I had to let the half-gallon well bucket stay down at the bottom a long time before it filled up with the sandy water. On the days that I was lucky, it would only take about an hour and a half to wait my turn, then pour water from the well bucket to our larger buckets until I'd collected ten gallons. I'd balance our two buckets on a pole that lay across my shoulders. During the walk back, most of the sand would settle to the bottom, but not all, before I poured this precious liquid into our family water tank. Even after all this, we had to boil whatever we used for drinking or cooking.

In the winter our community well had enough water, but that didn't mean that our troubles were over. Bathing was a chilly matter because we couldn't wash up inside without turning our dirt floor into a wet and muddy mess. Instead, we would collect water from our family water tank and bring it inside to boil. Then we would take it outside into the cold to mix with cold water, pouring the lukewarm mixture over ourselves to wash up. I learned to take the quickest bath in the universe, standing in the mud outside our small house, shivering in the cold.

Water. So many of us in America take it for granted that it will come hot out of a shower head as we get ready to go to our jobs. We pour ourselves delicious glasses of this pure, fresh liquid and rehydrate after exercise classes or a morning run. And in the summer, children can turn on a garden hose in their community and splash in the street. I wonder sometimes if the closeness in my village rose from our collective fear—life was always on the edge of being snatched away, if not by war, then by something as simple as a dry well.

* * * *

Considering how connected our community was, my mother's choice of a name for me was odd. The name she gave me at birth was Thản, which means *alone*. In addition to everything else I had to deal with, this name would announce to strangers that I should be avoided. On my first day of first grade we had to write down our name and birthday, and that was when I chose a new name. The name just came to me as I was filling out the form: Sau, which means "six" and is often used as a name in our culture. It does not mean anything special, but its primary benefit to me was that it didn't mean anything negative.

As a very little girl, I looked into the mirror and saw that I looked different from my brother and sisters, different from other kids around me, and I thought, *What is wrong with me?* I did not want to be Thản. I did not want to be alone.

Changing my name was not the same as changing *me,* or the father who made me different. And I wanted a father. Everyone I knew had two parents. My siblings had had a father, but he died, and that was an understandable reason for not having a father. Gradually I realized that even though I had the same last name as my siblings, we did not share the same father. But that was it—no further explanation. Nobody gave me a good reason why he wasn't there.

My weird looks and fatherlessness made me doubly alone, and that's how I had dealt with this issue—alone. My mom was too busy trying to bring in food and too caught up in her own misery to have time for me. She did not have time to explain why I was different and what I was going to experience from others. Most importantly, she did not talk to me about how to cope with being me. If I wanted to know about why I was different, I had to find out from other people. But in a country of sameness, telling a child that she is part American and her father is a black American was not easy for anyone to explain.

I spent my childhood avoiding confrontation. I didn't have the same childhood experiences as others, enjoying life, looking for the next adventure. Instead, I worried about what others would think about my actions. If I saw a group of people, I walked in a different direction so that I didn't have to deal with taunts, the possibility I would be called something horrible, or be told that I should go to America because I didn't belong in Vietnam. I longed to have a normal day, a day in which I could smell the flowers or enjoy the beautiful rolling hills. Instead, I was constantly nervous about what was coming. Was it an insult or a bullet? I hadn't forgotten the man in my sister's shop.

My hair became a problem no one knew how to solve. Where other girls may see a flower and put it in their hair to try to look beautiful, I couldn't—I was usually bald. No one knew how to deal with my kinky hair, especially when the weather was humid, and my mother didn't have the time to even try, so she would take me to the barbershop to have my head shaved. I still remember crying and throwing a fit, but I had no choice. My heart shattered every time she took me to sit in that chair, every time I watched them take out the clippers. I asked if they could at least leave an inch, but the answer was always no. My strange, shaved image in the mirror was just another layer of pain covering my heart.

Since the mirror told me almost nothing about who I really was, I began to piece together bits of information from other places. My identity, an explanation for what made me so different, was a puzzle I craved to solve. Without answers from my mom, I eventually pieced together some sort of story from neighbors and friends. They dropped little comments here and there, but no one really wanted to cover the entire story as they knew it.

A neighbor who was a distant cousin of my mother's told me what she knew about my father. My grandmother gave me another story that was relatively the same, but the shreds of information they shared did not make sense. From the snippets, I cobbled together a rough picture of my father and why I was different. My looks were strange, I learned, because I was half American, and—though we did not have this terminology— African American at that. My father was black, and I did not know what such words as "American" or "black" meant, but I knew that they were things that made me different. In time, I gradually understood that my mother and father had loved each other, and their union was no fling. And I would keep remembering the time I overheard the lady who had worked with my mother saying that he had come looking for us. I do not know if that was true, but it kept me going. It gave me the tiniest glimmer of hope.

Even though I had built up this working story about myself, I knew I had to keep trying to get the full and true answer from my mother. For several years she refused to answer my questions. She shut me out, and I found myself questioning everything about myself, even things about myself that weren't abnormal. My mother wouldn't answer even ordinary questions about being a girl and growing up.

Several years later, when I was thirteen years old, I sat at a window watching the rain come down, as it often did in the afternoon, and I looked at my big toe. For the first time, I noticed how much bigger it was than my other toes. The proportion didn't match the difference between my thumb and other fingers. I learned later that this was normal, but I didn't know that at the time, sitting by the window in horror, looking at my freak toe illuminated in the afternoon light. I thought, *This is just another thing wrong with me.*

I broke down and started to cry. Anger toward my mother filled me. *She did this to me*, I thought. I looked out the window at the rain coming down, tears streaming down my face, and I spoke to my mother.

"Why did you do this to me? Why do I look so different from the other children? Why don't I have a father?"

My mother looked at me, the sadness heavy in her face. I don't know why this was the moment she decided to break her silence—perhaps it was the rainy day, my tears, the gloom over our household—but she did.

"I went through all my difficulty all alone," she said. "I had no support from anyone, even family. Only the one neighbor would help me. If I didn't love you, I wouldn't have gone through all of the pain and trouble that you have caused me."

This was not the answer I was looking for. I waited for another rainy day, too rainy for her to go work in the fields. Nobody else was home, just the two of us. I found a quiet moment, when I could brush her hair for her.

"Mother, please tell me what is wrong with me. Why do I look in the mirror and see someone so strange? Why do I look different from you and my sisters and my friends? What is wrong with me? Did my father go away because of me? Who is my father? Why can't my father be here with us?"

She would not answer me at first. She could not look at me. She rose from the chair where she was sitting and began to fuss with kitchen tools. Suddenly, it was important to begin making our dinner. Anything so she would not have to face me.

"What is it?" I persisted. "Why do you keep secrets from me? Why do you want me to hurt like this?"

She could only answer my questions with a question.

"Don't you understand how good your life is, compared to the life I had as a child? Don't you know how lucky you are to be here at all?"

It would be years before I understood that she could have ended the pregnancy. Abortions were easily as shameful as having a baby out of wedlock, but far more unconscionable. Still, she would not tell me all the details. When I pushed, she broke down into tears and tried to reason away my questions with her own sorrowful childhood tales.

"My mother died when I was eight years old," she would tell me. "And then my father beat me every single day. My life was terrible. There is nothing you can say, nothing that happens to you, as sad and terrible as that. You have a mother who is with you every day, a mother who loves you and takes good care of you. I am sorry it is not better for you. I do my best for you."

She cried every time I brought up this topic. Perhaps she couldn't help her tears, perhaps her tears were a weapon—I can't really know. And the stories would begin again. "My life as a child was ten times worse than you have it. You shouldn't complain." Then she would list all of the hurt she had experienced. Her anger toward me would swell, and my unhappiness was never addressed. Every time. She only spoke of how it was hard for her to have me, not about my pain or my questions.

She told me long stories about how her mother's family beat my grandfather so badly they put him in the hospital because he wouldn't give them his money. After getting out of the hospital, he had to dress my grandmother in gold in order to divorce her. In Vietnam, that's a kind of reverse dowry, the only way a split can happen in that divorce-averse culture. The jilted bride's family wanted compensation for the humiliation, and if they had asked for a ton of rice or a cow, he would have had to give it to them. Instead, they asked for her to be entirely dressed in gold, from head to toe in gold, their last chance to squeeze money out of him.

My mother went on with her stories about how bad it was for her, how she went to live with her mother when her mother remarried. When my grandmother died in childbirth, my mother had to live with her father again. Since she looked like his ex-wife, he would always find an excuse to put down what she did and beat her. He hadn't forgotten what my grandmother's family had done to him. And on and on.

She was cooking while she told me this story, once again.

As I stared at the rain, I wondered, "Why, when I am suffering, do I get more pain dumped on me every time I ask this type of question?"

I came to the conclusion that I just need to keep my pain to myself, inside.

At this time I really needed my sister Tho. Perhaps she could have comforted me and helped me understand, but she was gone, and I had no one to turn to. My sister Huong could never comfort me the way Tho could. She was always deeply unhappy with my mom for having me. My mother's actions, Huong believed, made her a traitor to the Viet Cong, and she had to leave a good job working for them because of me. Worse, Huong resented my existence, for I was the evidence of that treason. My mother, by having me, cheated her out of a good life.

I can only guess how terrible it felt for Huong. But if Huong felt ostracized by our mother's shameful act and deprived of all the good fortune she believed she deserved, I believe it was several degrees worse for me. The torment an adult feels is different from the kind a child endures, and I would not wish either experience on anyone. Tho, I knew, would never resent me for being born.

Eventually I gave up dreaming and even trying to be happy. The only way to survive was to make myself go numb and accept whatever was thrown at me, no matter the reason.

* * * *

With each passing day, month, and year, my fear and anger continued to grow. Thank God my grandmother and a few very close friends were sweet to me. But people who didn't know me well would yell at me. "You are ugly. You are a freak." "Why don't you die or go to America?" And the worst was "You know, the government is sending people around to pick up American bastards like you to take them away and kill them. It's about time." The government could kill me, the government could hurt my family. There were good people who didn't blame me like this, but many others did. Strangers would tell me what they thought right to my face, and I became increasingly self-conscious and shy. I only wanted to hide. I thought at times I should just kill myself.

At school or on the street, as I walked to fetch water or any time I was out of our house, people stared and pointed; kids punched me, threw rocks, knocked me to the ground. As if I could've forgotten, they reminded me every day what a freak I was with my scary hair and dark skin. There was no attempt at politeness or pretending that my difference was not noticed. It was like I had a flashing neon sign attached to me. When I was thirteen, I even prayed that I would stop growing. I was scared that if I grew taller than others, I would be an even greater target.

Without my loving sister Tho there to comfort me and tell me I was good and that she loved me, I was adrift in my misery. All I could do was look in the mirror and wonder why, why did I look like a freak with my dark skin and my crazy curly hair? Everyone else had pale skin. Everyone else had silky, straight hair. What was wrong with me?

And even as frightened as I was about what the government might do to me, I felt grateful that no one forbade me to go to school. I loved learning and enjoyed the schoolwork. I was good at reading, writing, and math. The price of my education was high, of course. Each day brought a new piece of hell with the other kids in school.

Although being a walking target for abuse would be enough stress for any child, I also had to deal with the difficulties all children in Vietnam have when balancing school and home. Since we all had responsibilities at home, school was only a half day long with the remaining part of the day left for us to help our families. During sixth through ninth grade I went to the morning session. I walked thirty minutes to school and then home again. When I returned home my job was often to make lunch for my mother and the workers at our plot of land. I would take them their lunch and then usually stay to help them work in the field.

With those responsibilities, and all the housework I was required to do, homework would come last. More often than not, I rose at 3:00 a.m. to do my homework. My mother never sat down to help me. She did not believe in education, so it was up to me to finish my work before walking to school.

All students had to obey the teacher. My teacher was polite to me, but very strict. Skipping homework was not an option. Students who missed turning in homework once might be excused—once. But the second time, the student was whipped in front of the classroom with all their schoolmates watching. I wasn't about to risk that kind of humiliation on top of the kind my very existence brought me.

So with a lit candle, I stayed up at night to complete my homework and make sure that I understood the material backward and forward. At three o'clock in the morning, with my eyes tired and dry from little sleep as I studied my books, I felt all alone without Tho there beside me, helping me. So often I wished her back to life again, there by candlelight when the house was quiet.

Since Tho had been recognized and honored for her scholarship even though she had me for a sister, I had hopes that school would be a safe place because of the strict rules and merit-based rewards. I worked hard and did well, which had the unfortunate side effect of my teacher calling on me often since I usually knew the material. For other kids, this would be a matter of pride. I would soon find out that this only made the target on my back bigger.

During second grade, my teacher asked the class a question, and I and four other children raised our hands. The teacher called on me first, and I knew the answer and was praised. It felt good.

Then another student raised his hand. "Why should the American get a chance to answer the question first? She has no right."

Although I had become accustomed to rude comments, the student's disrespect, saying this to the teacher in front of the entire class, shocked me. The teacher yelled at the student, but several other students stood up and defended his opinion. The teacher made them apologize, which they did out of fear of punishment, but the shock had taken its toll. My defensive reflexes kicked into high gear as I wondered what this new danger would bring. I only had to wait until the end of school that day to find out.

As soon as I left for home, the students who had spoken up in class made it clear their apology was a lie.

"What makes you so special that the teacher always calls on you? An American?"

"You're nothing but a freak."

And the comments continued. They couldn't bear having a freak be better than they were at anything.

It was hard to get away from bullies like that. Our schoolrooms were tiny: sixty kids would be packed into one room about twenty feet by twenty feet. There were four gaping windows opened for circulation, and the floor was dirt. Depending on the day, our simple classroom was either a place of learning or a prison cell with no room to move. And just like any prison, the most serious damage was often inflicted outside the hearing of those in charge.

My attention during school became divided, since protecting myself from bullies became the more pressing need, and I began to lose focus in school. Eventually, as a matter of survival, I decided to do just okay at my lessons so that my head didn't stick up too high above the crowd. Once again, invisible meant safe.

The teachers never bullied me the way my peers did—in fact, they were kind and included me in anything to do with learning—but they excluded me from extracurricular activities such as singing. One particular time, when I was in fifth grade, my teacher announced she was going to teach us Tai Chi. There were fifty-three students in our class, but for some reason she said that she could only teach fifty-two children. I, of course, was the one who couldn't participate. I was very sad as I stood outside watching all my classmates learning the new thing. Then I sat, waiting for time to run by until the lesson was over. I cried, sitting there on the dirt floor, knowing I was *Thân*, not *Sau*. I was alone, not one of many.

After the lesson, somehow my teacher figured out what I had gone through as I waited for all of them to finish. She tried to comfort me, but nothing helped. My heart was already broken.

Over time, my skin thickened. I learned how to become numb. I knew deep in my heart that the treatment heaped on me was unfair. But because

I could do absolutely nothing about it, I found some switch inside myself to turn it off. Click. I just shut it out. At least most of the time I did.

One time after my brother beat me—the trigger this time escapes me—he went drinking with his friends. This time it got to me and I was furious. I wished that my brother would just die. I got angrier and angrier. "Yes, he should just die!" I said to myself.

The next morning I had to go work in the fields with my mom. Sometime later my brother and his friends walked by laughing. They said they were going to go fishing. My brother and his friends were lazy, so that meant fishing with land mines again. You trip a land mine, throw it into the river, BOOM, and up come fish.

For one "cast" my brother and his friends weren't quick enough. My brother lost a piece of his big toe and got a piece of metal in his neck. One friend lost an arm. The other friend lost his life.

While my brother spent the next two months in the hospital trying to heal and fight several cases of infection I tore up my insides, convinced that my wish had caused this. Even though we believed in karma, this was real and it scared me. As much as I hated my brother for the way he treated me, he was still my brother and a part of my life, and I did not want to lose him. Seeing my mom's misery over having her only son in the hospital only added to the guilt that I felt and it made me sick. I felt the need to confess to her that the day before the accident I had wished that my brother would die. Her devastation and exhaustion were so complete that she had no reaction to my confession.

All of this worry and guilt stirred up many memories. One of the memories was getting stung by a wasp on my finger, and with this new guilt it became clear to me that actions and thoughts both have a way of coming back to haunt me. This scared me to my soul. Since I already had a load of pain in my life caused by others, I had no desire to personally add more to my burden by wishing evil on others. I decided to never wish ill on anyone ever again. The cost was just too high.

* * * *

As each year went by, I learned not to hold Huong's resentment of me against her. People treated my family like trash because of my existence, and as a result they all resented the fact I was alive. I knew that, but I understood their frustration. Like me, they could do nothing to change the fact that I existed.

Looking back, I know that surviving that kind of emotional and mental torment built a strong backbone in me. Eventually the pain eased just a little. As I matured—and I had no choice but to mature early—I became tougher and more resilient. At some point I even became grateful for the lessons I was learning, because I realized that these difficulties were transforming me into a more perceptive and more capable person.

When I began to shift to a place where I resented my family's difficulty with me a little less, when I began to find more peace with my mother's decisions, I began to discover some moments in which I accepted myself. With that, I began to create my own hope, even if it was only a flicker of a candle flame trying to dodge the wind.

Four

"**C**an we go shopping this afternoon after school? I want to get some-thing to wear to the birthday party on Saturday."

"No," I tell Sydney. "We bought you four new things recently. You can wear one of those," I point out.

"But I need something new. Please!"

Sydney and I have these conversations frequently, usually in the car, just like today. We have a lot of time to talk every morning and every afternoon, five days a week. We live in a small community about thirty to forty minutes south of Fort Worth, Texas. I drive Sydney to her beautiful private school on my way to the salon where I see my first customer at 8:00 a.m.

The two of us travel the highway in complete comfort. I'm driving my small white Mercedes-Benz SUV that I've saved for. She's riding in the passenger seat next to me, dressed in her blue-and-red plaid school uni-form, playing with her iPad, listening to music. I look at this beautiful ten-year-old with her long, straight hair, her pretty face, secure in her idyllic world. And I shake my head.

"What? What's wrong?" Sydney notices my look of wonder. Then she gets it, or so she thinks. "Oh, okay. Okay."

She knows I'm about to tell her for the millionth time that she does NOT get it. I want to grab her iPad and pull up a photograph that does not exist. I want to show her a YouTube video that has not been recorded. I want her to see what life is like across the world, the dramatic difference between her life and my life at age ten. I wish she could understand the other side of the coin that was my childhood. But she cannot comprehend. Until I take her on the two-day series of flights required just to reach to the other side of the planet, to visit our primitive village in Vietnam, she will not get the harsh reality of my early life.

When Sydney comes home from school and finishes her homework, she's free to watch a movie or play games. She cannot understand that such things were never an option in my world as a child. Sitting around doing nothing, as kids here get used to doing, was unheard of in my childhood. Children in my world were busy all the time, taking care of something—we did housework and we babysat. Always. For most of my childhood, when my mother was working on the farm plot growing our rice and vegetables, I had to help as much as I could at home—and sometimes in the fields, too. My brother really wasn't someone who ever contributed, and my sister was living in her own home with her husband and family. I watched my sister's kids when I was just a little older than they were as toddlers. By the time I was eight, I was cooking and cleaning for our family. That is the way the world worked for us. It was how life was.

It was a surprise to me to find in America how normal it is for a girl to grow up and be so excited to turn sixteen and later to go off to college and to fall in love. None of that is typical of life in Vietnam. Here, we plan Sydney's birthdays as if they were Christmas, but it never occurred to me to be excited about a birthday when I was a child. That was a luxury we didn't indulge in, although I don't think my stone heart would have dreamed of celebrating anyway. Even when I got the chance to see a movie and saw someone fall in love, I thought, *Nothing like that could ever happen to me. That's not the life I will have. Work will be my future, and that's just how it is.* This beautiful girl sitting next to me as we drive to school has such a different life.

It's ironic that I've spent my life as a parent telling my two children, Scott (Phuoc) and Sydney, how hard they must work in school, how essential it is to focus on learning. I tell them of the worlds that a good education will open for them. My family's status had ruled out any important career for me, so education was not a roadmap I could follow. My goal at school was to not get beaten up or humiliated every hour of each day. School eventually quit being a chief concern for me. And sadly, I didn't have the chance to understand how much I was missing out on. My future was to be about finding some kind of a job that would help me keep a roof over my head.

But over and over Scott heard me say, and Sydney hears me say, that every day they go to school to listen, listen, listen to every word their teachers share. Take good notes. Focus on learning and taking every detail and storing it in your brain. Do they know how lucky they are to get these tools? And to have two parents who want a great education for them? My mother was happy to have me quit school and go to work with her. Does Sydney know how wonderful it is to learn at a safe place—in fact a prestigious private school where there are only nineteen to twenty students in the classroom? Does she ever think to appreciate that the floor of her classroom is made of tiles, not dirt?

Scott probably caught on to all of this at a very early age. He experienced our struggle in those early days here in America, and he remembers how hard it was. He wanted me to be there to walk him home or to see him play soccer after school. I couldn't—I had to work. My mother would walk him home from school. His sad face in the evenings broke my heart.

"I'm doing this for you. If I stayed home and didn't work, we would have no future. This is so you can go to college. This is so you will be able to pursue anything you want to do with your life."

Sydney hears us say that Mommy and Daddy sacrifice a lot so that she can go to the finest private school in town. We don't have a lot of money, but we have carefully budgeted and planned to make this work.

"You aren't going to school there because you are entitled," I say when Sydney starts to talk about all the things some of her school friends have. "It's because we think it's the best environment for you and will prepare you for the best future."

Because she attends school with some children who come from very wealthy families, she sometimes says she wants to grow up to live in a house like this friend or that friend. Sometimes she refers to someone who lives in a mansion, with a guard at the gate to the property and a staff to help run the home.

"When I grow up, I'm going to be rich and have a house like that," she says. And I want to scream. I don't, but I make sure she hears me.

"Do you think a life like that just happens? Do you know that you have to work to build the opportunity to have that life? Working hard in your wonderful school can point you to a good job where you can earn the life you want."

I've heard from some of my clients, too, about the mean girls. I never worried about Scott socially; I could see how easily he took care of himself. He's always managed friendships without much trouble. But I'm watchful about Sydney, making sure she has good boundaries with friends. She tells me that nobody has been mean to her; her friends seem to be kind, and I'm grateful. It would kill me if people were ever cruel to her.

Our drives to and from school and the city each day keep us connected. We talk about everything, something my mother would never do with me. I prepared her for her period to begin, which my mother didn't do with me. I didn't know what was happening until it happened, and even then, I was in the dark.

And whereas I had no choice but to learn to clean and cook, I want Sydney to do those things so that she's self-sufficient. I want her to be proud of being accomplished at everything. I'm teaching her to scramble eggs and to care for her belongings so that she's prepared to get out into the world when it's time for her to go to college and then be on her own. I taught Scott to balance his checkbook and lectured him endlessly about how important his decisions were—whether it was with drinking or with girls—and I will try to prepare Sydney, too. And though I can tell her over and over about the one new outfit I bought once a year to wear every single day of my life, with just one pair of shoes to last that year, can she really understand? Does she think I am crazy when I tell her that buying four new outfits at once is far more than enough? If she does, she won't say so. She knows how strongly I feel.

Even so, she will probably ask me again the day after tomorrow, just once more, about a new outfit for the party on Saturday.

Five

Although I started off in school with a determination to do well, the incident in second grade sent me down a path of mediocrity that had serious, long-term consequences. I didn't realize until ninth grade that my decision to underperform had flung me over a waterfall, one that would be extremely difficult to swim back up on my own. In other words, I was behind in my studies.

At first I was willing to work hard to make up for my bad decision all those years ago, but when I realized that I needed tutoring to help me get back on track, I knew I had a major problem. The few students I could call friends had either their fathers, older siblings, or other family members who could help them with homework. Unfortunately, since Tho had died, I no longer had anyone in my life who was either capable or willing to work with me. If it was going to happen, I would have to do it on my own.

Looking forward, I came to the conclusion that there was little to no hope for my future in higher education. I had let that opportunity pass me by, and I wasn't getting it back. This realization was a bitter pill, but one I had to swallow.

In Vietnam, education is important for younger children, but the system is selective for older children and teenagers. If you come from the right family, from people who work in government, you have a better chance getting a job in government—a respected job with good pay, by Vietnam's standards. And that's when you needed an extended education.

Because I was the product of an American, I had no chance of a government job; therefore a high school education would not benefit me in Vietnam. No matter how intelligent I might have been, I realized there was no future for me in school. I needed to go to work so I could figure out what my future could be. Curiously, some people kept telling me that because I was an American, I would find my future in America. To me, that made as much sense as going to Mars, so I did not see America as an option. Not for a while.

Right or wrong, I decided to stop going to school during the ninth grade.

＊ ＊ ＊ ＊

It was a day like any other Saturday and a shopping trip I made thousands of times. My mission was to buy some shrimp to cook with rice and vegetables for dinner for my mom and me. I made my way through the crowded open-air market, deep inside the steaming-hot, noisy mass of people, weaving around human roadblocks in the narrow aisles. The fish area, found at the center, was as congested and as pungent with briny seafood smells as ever. I searched for my favorite fish lady among all the fish ladies, packed in together as tightly as their plastic bins and woven baskets and large metal trays of fish.

Finding the lady and placing my order, I noticed someone next to me, looking at me. That wasn't unusual, but I sensed through the body language that it wasn't filled with the animosity and scorn I'd come to think of as normal. I looked into the woman's face, and it was one of concerned curiosity.

It was the principal from my school, a kind woman who had always treated me well.

"Sau, why haven't I seen you at school? Are you all right?" she asked me.

"Yes, I am fine. But I had to stop going to school. My mother needs me to help with her work and with everything at home."

"Sau, you must know that an education is important. You are a smart girl. You do well in school! You are one of the bright students. You belong in a classroom. Work can wait until later."

"Thank you," I told her, feeling a flush of pleasure at her warmth, and a hot rush of guilt. "But my mother needs me. The work is too much for her. I am all she has now."

"Please let me talk to your mother," the principal said, unwilling to give in. "Will she come see me at school? The door is always open to you."

I thanked her again and said I would try to persuade my mother. But the truth was, I'd thought long and hard already. I was too ashamed to say the truth out loud to the thoughtful school official: I had to drop out in order to find my own path. To stay in school would only be to delay the inevitable search for a future that school in our social system could never provide for an outcast like me.

I wondered how this educated, socially aware lady could be so mistaken. How could she not acknowledge the truth? How could she deny the fact that my American heritage only guaranteed that I could not have a secure future such as educated people enjoyed in Vietnam?

Not yet tuned in to a calling, my only possible work was in the fields with my mother. I'd done some of that with her already; it was always planting season for something—rice, sweet potatoes, yucca, all different kinds of vegetables. There were always seeds to be planted, watering to be done when the rain slackened, and plants to be harvested.

Our plot wasn't huge, perhaps just one acre, which was sad because our family had been big landowners for over a hundred years. But after the war, the government took over and allocated the land according to the number people in the family. Basically, we rented the land from the government, but the government was good about one thing: they made sure everyone had a plot of land, and each family was taught to be self-sufficient. If you needed to learn farming skills, you were taught how to grow everything you needed for your family to eat.

The downside of my new life as a farmer? It was always very, very hot and very humid. All the time. We all wore the woven, pointed hats called *non la*, or sometimes *non bait ho*, which kept the torturous sun off of our faces and necks or kept the rain from drenching our heads. To keep the sun from burning our arms, chests, and legs, we covered ourselves with lightweight, long-sleeved shirts and either loose pants or long skirts. The same clothes, every day. We washed and dried them overnight.

Days started very early in the morning, at first light, and lasted until dark. A fifteen-hour workday was usual. We would stop for lunch, and people who lived close enough might go home to eat at midday. The monotonous, tedious work never ended. At night, we would keep working, processing the rice by hand, for instance. You work, you sleep, and you work again. It was exhausting, but we did not know anything else, so it wasn't as though we would complain.

We were not religious people; my family didn't go to the Buddhist temple. But one day in the rice fields, I found my connection to God.

I was helping my mom in the fields. She ran out of fertilizer and as she stood up to go back home to get more, she noticed the sky and said, "It looks like rain, let's go home."

"I just have a few more rows to hoe," I said, "so you go and I will come home after I finish." And she left while I continued to hoe the dirt.

After a few minutes it started to rain, which wasn't that unusual in my part of the country, but I noticed the raindrops were unusually fat, splashing on my shoulders and my nose as I continued working. Before I could wonder why this rain was different, the clouds opened up.

It was as if ocean waves from the sky were heading right for me. I dropped the hoe. From past experience, I knew this could be a drowning kind of rain, something we call "running rain," like a flash flood. Fear washed over me as I began to make my way through the now blinding storm.

My trek home was normally a ten-minute walk, and not far from our house was a small creek. On a normal day, we had to wade through it, but during a running rain, this small creek would turn into a raging river that would sometimes overtake the rickety bamboo pathway placed there in case of a storm like this.

I pounded the road with all my strength, but deep down I knew there was no way I could make it home in time. My panic rose along with the floodwaters, and I imagined what it would be like to drown here, at the beginning of my life, while hope was still a covered light inside me.

Desperate for something to hold onto, I looked up at the sky and said, "*Troi con thuong con!*" Roughly translated, this means, "I know God still loves me."

I turned down the last stretch of path before our house. In the distance, the river that had overtaken the road rushed toward me, a mass of dirty water and debris. This was it, I thought. The end of my life.

Just then the main downpour of rain stopped about twenty feet to my left. When I reached the bamboo walkway, the swell of the flood was a foot away from me, but it stopped there, as if halted by divine intervention. I crossed the bamboo and made it home, drenched but alive.

Immediately the downpour began again. The storm continued for the next two days. Our whole town flooded, but God kept me safe.

* * * *

Though I was a help to her, my mom didn't want me to work forever in farming. She wanted me to go to tailor school, like my oldest sister, Huong, who was finding success in that trade. But nothing about sewing clothes appealed to me, not at all. I simply refused, but I knew in doing so I had to figure out something that did strike a chord inside me.

I searched for an answer and asked myself what it was that made me feel as though I were contributing to something valuable. What would feel most worthwhile to me? What inside me needed to connect with something important?

And the answer was as simple as looking in the mirror: I wanted to make women feel good about themselves. All my life, I was made to feel bad about myself because of my skin and my hair. I'd spent my life wanting straight hair and a different color skin, and I knew that shame over appearance led to misery. Once I prayed to an unknown God for straight hair. I wanted it so badly that one time I fried my hair by trying to straighten it with an iron stick that I heated in the stove fire.

If I couldn't change my looks, at least I could help other ladies with theirs. What I wanted—it came to me—was to help people feel beautiful. How special would it be, I thought, if I could help people enjoy what they see in the mirror? If I could make women look good and feel good, maybe it would help fill that emptiness inside me.

So my mother sent me to a trade school where they trained me to cut, perm, and style hair. After that, for practical experience, the school sent me to work in someone's shop. That way, I'd be ready to open my own shop. My mom's relative, Dieu, had a shop where they did hair, but it was in a nearby city. For a year I studied under her as an apprentice, riding my bicycle forty-five minutes each day to her shop and home again. I learned quickly and was ready to open my own shop in no time.

Back home in our city, my mom found a location on a cousin's property. We built my shop next to a supermarket, using money my mother had quietly stashed away while working for the Americans all those years ago. She was very smart with money and knew how to save, and she paid for the construction and all the work equipment I would need to run my shop. We were very fortunate; other people didn't have such an opportunity to start a business.

My shop was about twenty feet by twenty feet, complete with a kitchen in back. Right away, I had two students working with me, and I was teaching them what I had learned. If the foundation for my work ethic was laid when I was little, as I babysat and cooked and cleaned for the family, that integrity was cemented as I ran my shop. We began work very early in the morning and continued well after dark, because many of the working people couldn't arrive to get hair done until their workday had ended. We worked fifteen or sixteen hours each day, seven days a week. All year long we worked, taking off only a few days for the Vietnamese New Year.

The custom in Vietnam is to multitask, with one shop offering several services, so we also offered a wedding clothing rental business as well as doing hair and nails. Couples who couldn't afford to have their own wedding attire custom made would rent tuxedoes or suits for the groom and a number of dresses for the bride (a bride would wear one dress for the wedding and then change a couple of times at her reception). I would arrange all of their flowers, umbrellas, and shoes, and they would also pay me to do their hair for the wedding.

In time my business was flourishing, but there were still no products or equipment available to help me straighten my hair. So accustomed to the silky, straight hair of my customers, I still desperately wanted a different look. A friend of mine I'd worked with before came up with a novel solution one day: wear a wig.

Although we had both worked with extensions, neither of us had ever heard of anyone in Vietnam who used a full wig, and this concerned me. I didn't know if I could comb it. If I did, would it fall out?

She assured me the wig would last if I treated it right, but she needed an accurate measurement of my head to get started. As she spoke, I imagined flipping my lovely, straight, silky hair. And then she said something that took the smile right off my face.

"The problem I see is all of this," my friend said, pointing to my crazy, frizzy, full head of hair pulled back in a ponytail, which I wore like a big flower on the back of my head. "I'm not sure how short we need to cut your hair to get an accurate measurement."

Suddenly, the image of me as a young girl crying in the barber chair came back to me in a rush. In my memory, swaths of dark, frizzy hair fell around me as the barber followed my mother's stern instructions: "Shave her head." The humiliation of that moment washed over me, and I looked away from my friend.

"Are you all right? You look sick."

"Mmm. I think I will need to think a while and talk about this later."

I thought about her proposal for a long time. I wouldn't have hesitated to help one of my own clients if they needed a wig—it was my job to make them feel beautiful. But there was something awful about cutting off this part of me to get the measurement, even though I didn't like my hair. Perhaps that's what my young self knew long ago, sitting in that barber's chair. She knew that a woman's hair is a part of her self-image, and when the barber shaved my head that day, the act felt violent, insulting, and final.

Eventually, the unknowns of maintaining a wig, along with the memory of having my head shaved, was too much. I decided just to let my hair be as it was. I told myself I didn't care anymore if my hair was curly. I certainly wasn't interested in love or wasting time on courtship, so vanity didn't matter.

Despite my own reservations about the way I looked, I loved my job. In all, working in a salon was prosperous and important work, and I was thrilled. Most days would find me sitting at the front of the salon, greeting customers who came to tell me what they needed. My salon was very popular, and all from word of mouth. My reputation for doing wonderful things for people's looks was soaring. I was finding my place and my purpose at last.

Finally, after a lifetime of being told I was garbage, being made to feel as though I were less than nothing, I found out I was something after all. Nobody threw rocks at me anymore. Nobody told me I was terrible and that I should go away. Now, people loved the services I provided. They didn't care what my hair and skin looked like; I was someone who could make them feel beautiful, and they valued my skills. They wanted me to help them. I had transformed myself into a person of worth.

Six

Trang Nguyen first came to our family home with his brother, who was visiting our town on business. His brother knew some of my family, but it was the first time we had met Trang. Within minutes, Trang—a friendly, average-looking guy—surprised me with his boldness.

"When can I see you again?" he asked.

"Why would you want to do that?" I replied. The idea of dating couldn't have been farther from my mind.

"Because I like you and want to know you better!" His honesty was disarming. And pointless.

He wasn't taking no for an answer, though I kept giving him that same answer. For weeks and months. He'd visit from his town, which was an hour away, pursuing me, pestering me to date him, bringing me gifts, like a hat he had decorated for me. I found myself somewhat impressed that he had artistic talents, but ideas of love, dating, and marriage were completely irrelevant in my personal world.

In growing my thicker skin over the years, I had shut down all frivolous thoughts. In addition to purposely isolating my heart, I had no real understanding of romantic love. In Vietnam, love and sex are not discussed in the open, and my mom had never talked with me about this topic. I was unprepared for it. Here I was at age eighteen, passionate only about working as hard as possible to strengthen my business. Helping my mom was my only other focus. My brother, who spent time going back and forth between our home and Saigon, sometimes working in the coffee business and sometimes just doing nothing at all and living off of my mom, wasn't contributing. She needed me the most.

But Trang was thirteen years older than I was and overdue in finding a wife, so he went to work on my mom. And that, I'm sad to say, was the smartest thing for him to do. People in Vietnam do not get married because they're attracted to one another. They don't get married because they're in love. They marry because their families decide it's best.

And so our culture took over. Mom agreed to meet with his family, which was very wealthy at that time. She and Trang's mother struck up a friendship. And although I found his mother a phony who liked to show off their riches and make sure everyone knew how important their family was, my mother was won over. Once our families got together, they decided my future in no more than a couple of months.

"Trang is perfect for you and will make such a good husband," my mother said, trying her best to convince me. "His family is successful and he is a good match for you."

I stalled her, fighting with her for a few weeks. I thought perhaps because I had only one parent to defeat with my arguments, I might have some luck. My friends who dared fight with parents over these arranged marriages never stood a chance; one daughter against both a mother and father as opponents could never win.

"I have no reservations about Trang's character," I said to my mom, desperate to put years of feelings into word. "He seems like a good man. But I don't want *anyone*. The problem is that I have a hole in me. If I let myself have feelings for anyone, I'll get hurt. I know it. How can I be wedded to someone when I feel like this? I don't need a husband anyway—I have everything I want. A booming business, a good home here with you. What in the world can marriage give me that I need? Please, don't make me marry him—or anyone else!"

"Like everyone else, you will learn to love your spouse," my mother reasoned. "This has been the way for thousands of years and will always be how life is." And then she had to go for my jugular, to shore up her argument. "Don't you know how lucky you are to find someone who wants to marry you? You're half American. Your whole life you have been abused because you are so different, and now here is a good man from a wonderful family who wants you. *You.* How can you pass up this opportunity?"

In addition to the family-arranged marriage custom, I had another actor working against me and my wishes—my mother's shame. During my entire childhood, everyone always told me that no one would ever stoop so low as to marry me. To make matters worse, they said this to my mother in tones that made her feel as if someone had just spit in her face. After all those years, I'd become immune to the comments, but my mom took them to heart.

When Trang's parents told my mom Trang wanted to marry me, she felt as if she had just won the lottery. This was her one chance to get some relief from the constant burden of shame she had been carrying since the day I was born. Each time I tried to talk my way out of the arrangement, she would hear none of it. In one sense, I think she used the marriage negotiations, and eventually the marriage itself, as a means of revenge. So many around her said her shame could never be wiped clean—no one would want an abomination like me. This included her own sister, who refused to be with her on the day I came into this world. Now that she had proven them wrong, she wasn't about to let me take this victory away from her.

Feeling as if I would throw up all the time, I tried to live in my bubble of denial. Finally, I played my last card: I told Trang and his family that I could not bear to leave my mother alone. In Vietnam, every young wife has to go live with her husband's family and be the dutiful daughter-in-law who does all the family's housework. I told them this was impossible, that my conscience would not allow me to abandon my mother. Surely this would persuade them to find someone else.

"Sau, is that your worry? But this isn't a problem at all!" Trang assured me. "My family thought you might be concerned about that. Because I am one of nine children, we do not have to live with my parents at all. My other sisters-in-law will care for my parents and their home. We will live with your mother!"

I was out of options. And although I always respected our culture and its traditions and expectations, I felt betrayed and miserable. You cannot force someone to love someone else—but in Vietnam, that is simply how it works.

Like all Vietnamese weddings, my wedding to Trang was big. Between 150 and 170 people attended, including everyone either of our families knew. It was a two-day celebration, as is the custom, and I cried through every moment of it. My wedding photographs tell the whole story: In every single picture, I am sobbing. Not just weeping, but crying buckets of tears down my cheeks. What should be beautiful for everyone there was tragedy for me, and I made no secret of that. There was even a tornado during the celebration (a sign of things to come, of course!), so some of the planned festivities did not even take place. But at every turn, I was a sobbing mess in all my gorgeous, colorful gowns.

And though I was forced to be in close proximity, I did not warm up to Trang for a long time. He was patient with me, I will admit. He wasn't angry, but a bit sad, because I clearly didn't care much for him. All I wanted was to be at work. Finally, I began to feel sorry for him. Begrudgingly, I realized I had to figure out a way to like him a little bit, because in Vietnam, divorce was not an option. Nobody gets divorced.

Eventually, I relaxed and acted more like a wife. We had a son, Phuoc, in 1990, and I could divide my attention between my baby boy and my work, and more or less allow the marriage to progress on its own. Trang, I decided, could devote his attention to work.

A new devotion to work was much needed, because somehow Trang's family lost all of their money. Trang had worked in the past, before ever meeting me, but he'd never been in business for himself, and he'd lived mostly off his family. I believed he should follow my work ethic and find a career that allowed him to own his own business and be his own boss. It's the only thing that made sense to me. One of his brothers had prospered some years before in the duck-farming business, so I pushed Trang in that direction. Ducks brought steady income, the industry was stable, and my research showed it wasn't difficult.

Because Trang's family was broke, my mother and I financed the launching of a duck farm for Trang to run. This was the same year we had Phuoc, and I was satisfied that Trang had a good career. I went about my business as a new mom while also running my salon and wedding-supply shop.

I was horrified a year later to find that this duck farming business was falling apart. One moment I checked in to find it was running smoothly; the next moment it was bankrupt. Trang's selfish, greedy mother was stealing money out of the business when she thought nobody was looking. She was back to her old tricks, buying things to show off and make herself look important.

She left me no choice but to attack.

"How could your mother do this? My mother and I sank a healthy investment into your business, and your mother is wrecking it!" I railed at Trang, holding Phuoc, trying to keep him calm as my voice rose to near hysteria.

"She is my mother. She is my family. What is mine is theirs, just as it is yours."

"But she has no right to take money out faster than the business is earning. She is stealing from my mother and me! Without us, there was no business, and she ruined it."

Trang could not turn his back on his own blood.

"You cannot speak that way about my family. You are wrong. You will see."

He pretended to be shocked, but he obviously wasn't angry. This made me even more suspicious.

"Do you think I am stupid? My mother is my family, and my family is my honor. Without my mother's support, no business was possible. This was betrayal, this was theft. Your family has ruined my family and its reputation." He had no idea how hard it had been to restore that family credit card, the one that I had ruined by existing.

But Trang blindly believed I was wrong, mistaken somehow. In my devastation, I felt a blackness growing in my gut like a cancer. Here I was, with a precious newborn son—and a new family that had humiliated my family and me, casting a fresh and heavy shroud of disgrace over us. To be so thoroughly deceived—to have trusted and been wronged by in-laws and shown to be a fool in the process—was a whole new shame to bear.

Whatever hope I had begun to feel, whatever tenuous grasp I thought I might have had on a good and decent and rewarding life was slipping away at lightning speed. My mother bore the disgrace with me. How I longed for someone to just love me. How I missed my beautiful, dead sister, who gave me that sense of hope, so long ago.

I muddled through days working and tending to my son, ignoring

Trang all the while. This went on for a long time, until one day he came to me, humbling himself. I saw real pain in his face, perhaps humiliation, as well.

"Sau, I owe you an apology. I have learned that you were right. My family lied to me. I couldn't believe my mother would do this to us, but I found out she did exactly as you said. I hope you can forgive me for not believing you."

I knew he was sincere; I could see that it hurt him that his own flesh and blood would wrong him and his new family. But although I believed him, my heart was dead to him. I felt no conflict; I wanted to be finished with him, utterly and completely. Too much damage had been done.

The time soon came for me to tell my father-in-law exactly how dishonorable I knew him and his family to be.

"After I trusted you and your wife and your family, after my mother and I opened our hearts and our savings to you to help your family, you betrayed us. You destroyed our honor."

My father-in-law just looked at me. He had no response. I could not see any remorse. Though my husband felt ashamed, his own parents would not take responsibility for their actions. I was so ashamed that I couldn't even tell my closest friends what had happened. Shame for this kind of dishonor is deeply rooted in our culture. While we were Vietnamese who weren't wealthy, we kept great stock in our pride and reputation. And that's what I felt this family had destroyed for my family.

And that's when I made up my mind to go to America. Since I was a child, people had sneered at me and said, "Why don't you leave? Go be with your people, you belong in America." And for the first time, I believed that was exactly the right thing to do.

* * * *

Finding a time when we were alone, I explained my decision to my mother. We were in our home, putting away dishes in our kitchen after dinner. My voice was quiet, calm, and firm.

"I am leaving Trang. He broke my heart, he wrecked my trust. I have no love for him or his family. I want to leave him behind and take you and Phuoc. We will get as far away as possible."

My mother was shocked; her face going slack and pale. She looked as though I had knocked the wind out of her.

"Sau, no, no, this is not possible. How could you even consider this, after you have worked so hard to build your wonderful business! I have saved and worked and kept us moving forward. How can we run away from that?"

"I am ready to leave my friends, give my business away to someone who needs it, and never come back to this country. I will do anything I must to leave all of this behind us. I have to get away from Trang and all the misery he brought to our door. I have been kicked down enough."

So I began my preparations to leave. Making the decision, believing in my decision, gave me an enormous sense of relief. I turned my face toward a life in the United States as someone turning her face up to the sun after too many years in a prison cell. The possibility of shedding my shame and finding my true identity brought that flicker of hope alive again, the one that had been extinguished all those years ago when Tho's life was blown away by an exploding land mine. On that candlestick deep inside me, a flame was burning.

Seven

In early April 1975, Saigon was falling to Communist troops from the North and rumors spread that southerners associated with the United States might be massacred. Out of fear for our safety, my mom didn't dare put my father's name on my birth certificate. She destroyed all photos and mementoes associated with him. There were times in my life that I wanted to deny that I was Amerasian, a descendant of a Vietnamese parent and an American parent. But as I made plans to go to the United States, that blank space on my birth certificate was no longer a stumbling block, but a pathway.

Amerasians were born to Asian women and American men (usually in the military), and most of the Amerasians in Vietnam had neither contact nor support from their fathers. At this time, there were a lot of children like me, more than twenty-five thousand, born of a Vietnamese mother and an American military father, wanting to come to America. In 1980, Connecticut Congressman Stewart B. McKinney called the American government's abandonment of these children of war a "national embarrassment" and urged fellow Americans to take responsibility for them.

The American Homecoming Act of 1987, effective in 1988, helped Amerasians remaining in Southeast Asia immigrate to the United States. It is believed that twenty-six thousand men and women, along with as many as seventy-five thousand of their relatives, came to the United States to live.

So when I was twenty years old, I began the process that would bring me and my family to America. The way it worked, the Vietnamese government let Amerasians like me apply for a refugee application, but we had to give up our citizenship before we had the interview that would determine if we were allowed to leave and become American residents. So it was a big gamble because if I didn't pass the interview, I didn't have a country. I would be an outlaw.

When Trang realized I was serious about leaving him and Vietnam, his repeated apologies for his family's deception became more insistent. He was desperate for me to believe him and not shame him by ditching him there. Then my mom, unwilling to be any party to the shame of divorce, tugged at my heartstrings.

"What are you going to do when your son asks who his father is? What will you say to him? Did you not plead with me for much of your early life to tell you about your father? Did you not ache from not having a father at home with us? I did not keep you from your father. How can you keep your son from his father?"

She was right. Growing up without a father was very hard for me, and I really wanted my child to have a father. I struggled terribly with the idea of taking my son away and putting him in the painful situation of not knowing his dad.

Soon Trang was begging me, pleading with me: "I will be a better husband! I will be a better father!" He so wanted to start over again with me in America. I could not let Phuoc have no father, so I gave in.

In November 1991, I finally submitted my application to the Vietnamese government in Hue, the major city nearest my town, and then they sent it along to Saigon (which was by then renamed Ho Chi Minh City, but we still think of it as Saigon). Things happened pretty quickly. In February 1992, I got a letter that directed my entire family and me to Saigon for an interview with the Vietnamese government. In person, they conducted a DNA blood test, revealing that my father is American, and proving my privileged status as an Amerasian.

But clearly, I was recognizable to experts as half American, and I did fine in that interview. That summer, I went back to Saigon for another interview, this time with the American government.

I tried very hard to be calm on the outside as I approached the building, but my insides were jumpy. Inside, the halls were bright and clean; the offices were well-lighted and cool, unlike most of the sweltering buildings everywhere that were just as hot inside as outside. Here, in the air-conditioned lobby and various offices, there were American flags hanging on wooden poles and framed photographs of the thin-faced man I would know later as the first President Bush.

The interviewer was a pleasant, middle-aged man who spoke in a kind tone. I don't know his name, and I cannot remember if anyone told me what his title was. I was nervous, wishing so deeply for everything to go well. We talked about my family and my readiness to be in America. I wanted to answer everything correctly.

And then the interviewer asked a question I didn't expect, one that would reveal a new dimension in the world of my self-esteem, a part of me that would soon open in a way I would have never imagined.

"I hope you do not mind if I ask you an unusual question," the American interviewer asked me, communicating easily and politely in Vietnamese.

"I do not mind," I replied. I wasn't about to complicate my interview if I could help it. He was free to ask whatever he needed to know, as far as I was concerned. And who was I to say what is an unusual question? None of this was *usual* to me.

"I am curious why you wear white makeup? Your skin is more of a brown color. It seems odd that you would wear white makeup on skin that is darker."

I stared at him for a moment, not comprehending the question at first. And then I realized he thought I had a choice. So I answered, "This is the only color of makeup we have in my town and in my salon. I do not have any way to acquire any other color makeup. There is no makeup for my skin color."

He paused, and smiled. And then he said something I will never forget: "Where you're going, you won't have to wear the white makeup anymore."

He was telling me I was going to America, where I would find the right makeup for my face. The candle in my heart flamed brighter.

After this interview, my life changed forever. From this moment on, my family and I were essentially wards of the United States, although we still lived in Dam Sen. Everything, from room and board to all transportation for our numerous appointments, was funded by the United States government. Before this moment, my family and I had to work hard just to scrape by. Now this far-away place, this country that was still a stranger to me, was taking care of us.

We would leave Vietnam in November 1992.

Eight

Overnight, I became someone with distinctive appeal.

As a half-American child, I was an outcast from society, but when the American government decided to start making residency available in that Promised Land for children of American soldiers, my position skyrocketed. This irony was not lost on me; I thought it was amazing that while I was below worthless as a child, now I had great value. People in my shoes were immediately enviable—something I had never, ever been. Suddenly, Vietnamese who desperately wanted to leave the oppression and poverty in our country would try to "buy" someone like me. In other words, people would pay someone like my mother and my siblings to stay home in Vietnam so that they could pose as my relatives and escape Vietnam with me. That's how dramatic this new movement of Amerasians immigrating to the United States truly was.

Our initial plan for the move to America included me, my husband Trang, our son Phuoc, my mom, and my brother. But it was not to be. My brother, Huy Van Le, was older than twenty-one, and the recently changed rules prohibited any sibling over twenty-one from joining the Amerasian emigrants. He would be left out of the move and was devastated by the news. He and my mother were close, and I grieved for him, and especially for the distress this caused my mother.

Though my brother had been difficult with me as I grew up, I had forgiven him for the beatings and humiliation. I didn't want him to be crushed, but I had no choice in how this was turning out. I tried to help out the only way I could.

"Brother," I said to Huy Van the day before we left, "I wish I could help you. I wish I could control this, but it's all out of my hands. All I can do is give you what little I have."

"What? What can you do but take away my family?" Huy Van often tended to feel entitled. He always thought my mother and I could do more for him. Nevertheless, I couldn't imagine how lost he must have felt.

"I know you're upset because I'm taking mother away with me, but it is the best thing for her. I can care for her as she grows older, and I need her to help with the baby when I am working. So please, take this as my gift to you."

I handed my brother a gold necklace that I loved very much, a beautiful little thing I had bought to remind myself of my hard work and success. It was valuable, and he needed it more than I did. I also gave him a little bit of money I had left after paying for travel expenses not covered by the Americans.

"We do not know what is ahead of us. We do not even know if we really will reach our new home safely. And if we do, we don't know if we will ever see you again. So I want you to have this," I said, surprising myself when tears stung my eyes. I don't know if I felt like crying because I was saying good-bye, perhaps for the rest of my life, to my only brother, or whether it was because of my fear and uncertainty about what might lie ahead.

* * * *

We began the transition. First, the American government directed us to move into a modern American facility in Saigon called Dam Sen, funded by the American government, where they begin the emigration process for Amerasian children. While we were there, we underwent medical care and checkups; the Americans bought our plane tickets, and we prepared to move to our new country.

In November 1992, we left Saigon for the Philippines, where we lived for six months. The system for moving to the United States in those years required that we spend time in something like a halfway house, where we could learn American customs. The orientation period was helpful in many ways, as we would quickly learn.

The process was somewhat like going to continuing education classes. Classes with different instructors gave us English lessons. Other sessions taught us how to shop in a mock supermarket, showing us how to pay for things with American money. We had sessions on the American banking system. In classes that covered basic life skills, we learned how to use a gas stove.

In my spare time, I gathered clients who wanted haircuts and styling, so I was able to earn some money. In fact, during the six months we were there, I saved cash that allowed me to buy us extra food, toiletries, and accessories, plus a few treats for Phuoc (Scott). As we were leaving, I traded my Philippine money in for American dollars, enabling me to arrive in the United States with twenty dollars in my pocket.

Although that twenty dollars seemed powerful in my pocket, I brought something with me that was far more essential to my survival in my new home. Our time in the Philippines marked a powerful turning point in my

Sau, Phuoc (Scott), and Sau's mom in the Philippines celebrating
with people in their barracks the news that Sau's family had a sponsor.
Author's collection.

life. During this interim phase of our journey, my roots in my Christian
faith sprouted and grew.

In Vietnam, my family was not religious. Although there was a Catholic
church in our town and there was Buddhism, we practiced neither. Yet
even though we were not actively religious, we have always prayed to God,
the higher power that makes all life possible. Finally, I would learn what
the Bible was, and I learned to worship in the Christian faith.

Sau and her ESL teacher celebrating Sau's passing one of her many skills tests. *Author's collection.*

Given the chance to learn more, I was fascinated. I found I hungered for a structured, formal sense of God, that I craved the means for worship. When sessions were offered in Christian church lessons, I jumped at the chance. Though I couldn't read English yet, we heard stories from the Bible. And though I would not understand for several years that the Bible is a series of books and lessons and history, I gravitated toward the truths I realized had been missing from the spiritual space inside me. We learned about church services and a sense of togetherness I would one day understand as fellowship.

Meanwhile, we waited to find out who would be sponsoring us for the move and settling into life in America. For the family of an Amerasian like me, the move to the United States happens because there is a partnership or agreement between the American government and a pool of sponsoring groups, which are typically churches. If the Amerasian had no friends or family in the United States, there would be an effort to get sponsorship for them through those channels. We knew no one, and I was willing to go anywhere. I didn't know there were fifty states to choose from, and I had

Sau with a fellow Amerasian in the Philippines.
Author's collection.

no idea that some were cold and some were hot.

We got our sponsor letter about six weeks after we arrived in the Philippines, which was wonderful. It was one of the times in my life where I felt—again, we had no real religious practices where I came from—sure that a power high above me was looking out for me, making a plan happen for me. And sure enough, there was a sponsor in Fort Worth, Texas: Travis Avenue Baptist Church, which wanted to sponsor me and my family. We had the right to refuse if we wanted to go to California or somewhere else. I didn't care what was in Fort Worth; I was just very excited.

We understood this letter coming when it did was a very good sign. We befriended people who had left Vietnam in boats and somehow made it to the Philippines, where they waited for ten to twelve years or more to find sponsorship. They had been there for so long that they learned to read and write English, so they were able to do a lot of research for us. I was encouraged because they told me that in Texas, the weather was good and there were bus services and job opportunities.

So I was grateful, happy, and ready to make plans to move to Texas.

We were given a travel date. Our trip to America would cost us $3,200, an amount in the form of a loan that we would repay over time.

As we prepared to leave Asia for our future in America, the timing was perfect for learning how to walk on my new path of spiritual discovery. I felt a connection and sense of belonging to something much bigger than myself, something huge and powerful and important. The fear and torment of my early life, the recent family disgrace, and even the long-ago sadness and loneliness attached to losing Tho seemed far more bearable. Even the anxious uncertainty of the unknown life ahead of us felt somehow more manageable with this source of light and caring that I felt in embracing my new faith. Hope finally became something tangible, with God directing and protecting my family and me.

Nine

We finally boarded our flight for the United States on June 2, 1993. I'd never been on an airplane, and I was miserable for the nearly seventeen hours of flight. All the things they taught us to do in the Philippines did not include how to unbuckle my seatbelt on the plane. I didn't know how to get out of my seat, and I didn't know how to ask for help, so I thought there was something wrong with my seat and the airplane. It was a long, difficult trip. Thankfully, Phuoc was a good baby and traveled well. We all stayed healthy. I was grateful that all of us arrived in good shape.

We arrived in Los Angeles, and from there we took a three-hour flight to Texas, arriving at DFW Airport about midnight. Early summer in our new home was very hot, even at night, and the weather in Texas suited us perfectly.

Arriving on the same plane was another Vietnamese family of four, a single mother with three children, one of whom was a young Amerasian woman like me. Their path to immigration was similar to ours, but we hadn't met in the Philippines. Standing near the baggage carousel, I spoke with the mother, Hong Pham, who said her family's sponsor was the same church as ours in our new hometown of Fort Worth.

Right away, we all noticed a Vietnamese man walking toward us. With a shy and slight smile, he introduced himself as Ba Thong, explaining that he represented Travis Avenue Baptist Church. He'd be driving us to our home, but I'd quickly learn that Ba, our liaison, would be much more to us than a driver. He was our connection to everything we would see or do. Our eating, sleeping, and all manner of acclimating would come under his guidance.

Ba arrived from Vietnam and learned his way around Fort Worth a few years before we did. We had much to learn. He had already conquered what we faced, but his transition to his new home had been difficult. He was a refugee who left Vietnam by boat and was one of many thousands who were helped by American war-relief groups that developed connections with sponsoring churches in the United States.

His understanding of how things worked and expertise in adapting to life in this strange new land would quickly become our lifeline to a functioning future. His friendly face would become one of my favorite sights in the days and weeks to come. Soon I would understand that he was one of many angels God sent to help my family and me.

Our drive from the airport to our new neighborhood on what's called the South Side of Fort Worth probably lasted only thirty or forty minutes, mostly along one ribbon of modern, concrete freeway after another. Just before we reached our part of town, we passed the high-rise buildings—many of them outlined in permanent lighting—of downtown Fort Worth. I barely noticed; I doubt any of us did. The dark of night cast a shroud over everything, and we were all bone-tired from endless travel and dazed at the prospect of arriving in a vast unknown land.

As he drove us, Ba explained that our two families would be sharing a house for a short time. My family's home was ready to be occupied, but the nearby house meant for Hong's family wasn't quite ready. Ba said the four Trans would be with us for just a night or two at most.

When we arrived at the house on McCart Avenue that the church had rented for us, we didn't have the opportunity to take in surroundings that would be plain to see in daylight. We didn't yet realize we lived on a busy thoroughfare in a crowded neighborhood.

Inside the house, we put down our few bags and looked around. We were speechless. Later I would come to understand that our temporary lodging was the most basic, no-frills house, but to our two families, it was easily the most luxurious arrangement we had ever seen.

He led us to the kitchen, which had a stove like the one we learned to use in the Philippines. And there was the big box that kept food chilled, an item nobody we knew had ever used in Vietnam. Ba opened the door of this big box—which I would learn was a refrigerator—and showed us all the food inside that had been prepared for us by volunteers at our sponsoring church. We had everything we needed for a couple of days, he promised.

Assuming that in our exhaustion we would be ready for sleep, Ba bid us good night and said he'd check on us the next day. The eight of us watched him leave. Then we stared at each other. What now?

Other than catnaps on the airplanes, we hadn't slept in two days. But nobody, other than baby Phuoc, could sleep. Nervous energy or adrenaline, whatever—we couldn't unwind.

It was very quiet outside and dawn was still hours away. I could see in Hong Pham's small, round face and those of her son and daughters that they were as scared and anxious as we were. We all talked in nervous bursts through the night.

"We are really here! It seems like a dream, but I know I am awake," I said to Hong. "I wanted to come to America so desperately, and now I am here, and yet I cannot believe it is true."

"I have prayed for our safe journey and prayed that we would find someone here who is good to us," Hong said, her dark eyes damp, her small hands gently folded in her lap. "I think our prayers are answered." I kept looking around the house, trying to visualize our lives fitting into this strange structure.

Trang saw me staring at a wall. "Sau, what is wrong? We are here. We are okay. This Ba will help us figure things out," he said, trying to be of some comfort to me.

"I know," I said to my husband. "I am so grateful that we are in a place where there is a floor. There is carpet. There is no dirt floor for us now."

Hong listened, nodding her head. A big smile covered her face. "And when I look up, I don't see sky from inside the house. There is a roof over our heads."

My mother could not stop looking at the bathroom, with its bathtub and shower—and a very complete toilet. "There is a cover on the toilet!"

After marveling over and over at both toilet seat and toilet lid, we walked back and forth in the very short hallway between the two bedrooms. With closets in them. We agreed that our American palace was very nice, indeed.

"I wonder if our house will be this nice," Hong Pham mused aloud. "If it is this large, I wonder how we can fill the space."

Hong, Trang, my mother, and I talked for hours about the size of the house and how much more space it afforded us. It was much more than we'd ever imagined. Then, an idea occurred to me. I turned to Trang and Hong with a new energy, and Trang looked at me with a look that said, *What is it now?*

"The church has promised to help us find jobs," I began, "but we do not know how much money we can earn here. We don't know how long it will take us to repay the travel loans."

"Yes, but there is a grace period of—what did they tell us? Three months?" my husband asked.

"That's right, but we want to do more than repay the debt. We want to save money. There are so many things we will need. I think I know how we can stretch our money, how all of us can get ahead more quickly."

"All of us?" Hong was all ears.

"We, all eight of us, are in this new world together. We have so many similarities in our lives. We should stick together and help each other. If we all stay together in this house, we can split the rent and make our money go farther. We can accomplish our goals more quickly!"

In just a few hours, our two families saw how comfortable we all were with each other. And where we came from, it was nothing for eight people to live in a small space together. The Vietnamese way is very communal; togetherness is customary among families and neighbors, so this made perfect sense to us. Half of $325 per month was sounding very good to

Hong's family and to mine.

Finally feeling as though we had made an important life decision, we felt more settled—safety in numbers and all that. Too tired to talk any more, we drifted off to sleep as the sun began to rise.

A few hours later, I awoke with a start. It was daylight—and what was that all that noise? I looked out the window and was startled by a sight I hadn't, for some reason, expected.

Our house was situated on a very busy, four-lane street. About twenty-five or thirty feet from the window, past a small lawn and on the other side of a strip of concrete I'd learn was called a sidewalk, cars of every shape, size, and color whizzed past. Two lanes went one way, two went the other way, and every car seemed to go really fast. Every now and then a bus would come along. I only saw an occasional person walking along the sidewalk. There was nobody on bicycles.

In Vietnam, the busy streets were loud with a profusion of buses and small cars, but we were accustomed to seeing thousands of people on a single street in a single day on motor scooters, motorcycles, bicycles, and still far more on foot. But we didn't have houses so close to the busy streets. The sight was surreal to me. Many years later I would record an Anthony Bourdain TV show segment in which he visited my hometown. I wanted to show all my new friends in America how completely different my Vietnamese home was from the place I found myself that first morning in Fort Worth. The culture shock could not have been more extreme.

Eventually, I tore myself from that window to find everyone else. I discovered my mother, Trang, and Hong's family all in the kitchen, all looking confused and a little desperate. Like me, everyone was famished. During the long night before, we'd talked about being hungry—we hadn't really eaten much since leaving the Philippines—but we didn't see anything in the strange refrigerator that we recognized.

"Surely Ba would leave us food we can eat! He seems so nice," my mother said.

"Does the church know what we eat?" my husband wondered aloud.

"Maybe we just need to look at the food more carefully. Maybe there is something we will find familiar," Hong suggested.

But nobody was brave enough to investigate. Finally, I decided to give everything another examination.

I reached into the refrigerator and grabbed one of the glass casserole dishes. I peeled back the layer of aluminum foil and then a layer of plastic wrap. Inside, a bumpy yellowish mass sat there.

"What does it smell like?" my mother asked.

I sniffed tentatively. "Nothing. No, it's something. But I don't know what."

"Does it smell bad?" Hong asked.

"I've never smelled anything like this, ever."

We all just stared at it. I covered it up again and returned it to the shelf in the fridge and tried something else. Pulling out another glass dish and uncovering it, we discovered a mass of stringy something that sort of looked like the glass noodles we eat in Vietnam. But atop the strands was a thick red sauce, nubby with something brown, all covered in a latticework of white something.

Much later we would come to know macaroni and cheese, spaghetti with meat sauce, and other casseroles as delicious homemade American dishes. But never had we encountered foods made with butter, cream, or cheese. Dairy is not part of our culture in Vietnam. All we knew were very simple, plain foods. All we'd ever eaten was a diet of rice, fish, chicken, vegetables, and fruit.

We just could not eat these odd, foreign creations. It all looked and smelled so bizarre to us. So we simply did not eat.

Ba had told us the night before he'd take us to a Vietnamese grocery store on our first full day in Fort Worth. We knew he was working during the day, however, and we didn't want to wait any longer. The idea of waiting until he was finished with work in the evening was impossible to us. We needed to find something we could eat. So we went walking.

In Vietnam, we walked everywhere, so walking in search of a grocery store was no big deal. I still had that twenty dollars in my pocket, and I thought, *Let's go find something we can eat.* So with Phuoc on my hip, we all walked about eight blocks up McCart Avenue to a supermarket on Seminary Drive. The thrill that filled us at finding the store overwhelmed us; we were absolutely giddy. But it was short lived.

Entering the store, we stopped dead in our tracks. The lessons in the Philippines would not help us now. We had only shopped in mock stores and they were not arranged like this supermarket. It also wasn't set up like the markets at home, so we didn't know what to do. Where were the stalls? Where were the booths in rows, with vendors selling individual items? We saw apples, bananas, carrots, cucumbers, peppers, and all kinds of food we knew, and we wanted them all so badly. We were really, really hungry.

"What do we do?" I asked Hong, who was clutching my mother's hand. The two of them stared at the vast array of produce, looking as though they might both burst into tears.

"Who do we pay?" asked my husband. All of us looked around to see what the other shoppers were doing.

Everyone moved about the store with confidence, picking up items they were gathering in their handbaskets or the larger, metal wire baskets on wheels. We could not understand checking out with a cashier. Here, there were no vendors taking money for the fruits, no vendors taking money for the cabbage and other vegetables.

We walked around, up and down the aisles of shelves with neatly arranged items. I was sure I'd burst into tears when I saw packages of rice, lots and lots of rice. We saw chickens in plastic wrapping in the chilled case.

"How can we get the chicken? The rice? If we pick it up and put it in our basket, will they think we are stealing the food?" my mother moaned softly. Hong patted her hand and shook her head.

A kindly looking woman in the store saw how confused we were, and I think she wanted to help. She found an older man, tall and thin with dark hair and gray at the temples. He had on a blue shirt with a name tag; he was probably the manager. They were smiling and speaking in a friendly way, wanting to help. But they didn't speak Vietnamese; we didn't know how to make them understand what our trouble was.

Frustrated and exasperated, I went into flight mode. "Let's not get in trouble, we don't want to go to jail," I said, fighting back tears.

So we walked back home, hungrier than I have ever imagined being. I was weak from needing to eat, and Phuoc was fussy, surely reacting to my bleak mood, and all eight of us were cranky and tired. Yet one thought burned through to the surface of my muddled head: It's so strange that during the time we spent in the Philippines, we worked hard to absorb all the lessons being given us. The whole process we experienced in the Philippines was specifically designed to keep us from suffering terrible culture shock. And now that we had arrived in America, we were drowning in culture shock. All I could think was how ironic it all seemed.

When we reached our block and were three or four houses away from our new home, Ba came running frantically toward us. The face we'd seen as calm and sure the night before was awash in panic. And we were thoroughly grateful to see him. Our combined energies created quite a bit of pandemonium in the conversation.

"Thank God you're okay!" Ba said. "I came by to check on you and you were gone! I didn't know what to think. I didn't know what happened to you!"

"Thank God you're here!" I said. "We are starving! We went to the grocery store to get food and didn't know how to buy anything!"

"How can you be hungry? There is a refrigerator filled with food!"

"We can't eat it," Hong said. "We don't know what it is. We need food we know."

Ba closed his eyes, nodded his head, and clasped his hands together in relief and understanding. He smiled.

"Ah. I thought in the Philippines they would introduce you to American food. I did not know you would find this food so strange. Trust me. You will come to love it. But for now, let's find you the food you know how to cook."

Ba's patience with us became evident that very day. He drove us to the supermarket and showed us how to load everything in the shopping cart and check out with the cashier. Even though we did finally learn how to shop in the American supermarket, it was still too confusing to find the food we wanted, and we knew we could find more of the Asian noodles and the things we were used to in the Vietnamese store. It would be a long time before Tom Thumb became our go-to.

For two years or more, we would still walk to the Vietnamese grocery store we found on the other side of Interstate 35, which was much, much farther away. Ba said he would take us, but we didn't like bothering him for every single thing. Though we wanted to adapt to our new home, there were some habits we wouldn't easily leave behind. Walking would remain a constant for us.

Ten

During that first week we were in our new home, I woke each morning at daylight with the same thoughts racing through my head. I felt a sense of urgency inside, a need to get busy. For as long as I could remember, I had depended on myself. I enjoyed being responsible, useful, resourceful, and productive—habits since childhood. I felt the same drive wake up as soon as I did—my need to be industrious right away.

My husband, who hadn't worked as hard as I had over the years, had trouble understanding my anxiety. I was bathing and dressing Phuoc on our fourth or fifth morning in Fort Worth when Trang asked again why I was so restless.

"We are here in America, but what are we doing?" I asked him. "We have achieved this much, just getting here, but that doesn't mean we are supposed to sit back and do nothing."

"But the sponsorship program gives us three months to adjust. We aren't required to do anything yet but look around and get to know our new surroundings."

I looked out the window, still shocked at the profusion of large and small, old and new cars zipping past our house, and still astonished that nobody walked anywhere. I felt a rising surge of worry that I didn't know anything about how the world worked in this strange new city.

How would I learn to drive a car? Where would I get a car? How much would it cost? How long would it take to save that money? The questions roared around in my head, but I knew that to share them with my family would get me nothing but eye rolling. As I walked with Phuoc on my hip into the kitchen, I shook my head, unwilling to say much more.

Trang was right about one thing: I'm the one who looks too far ahead. I'm the one who is impatient.

My mother joined us at the kitchen table by this time. "What's wrong, Sau? Aren't you glad we made it here? Isn't our new house perfect for us? We are safe. We are well."

"Yes, of course. But I don't know what to do with myself. I want to know what our next steps are." What I didn't say was that I couldn't figure out if we would really ever belong here. Had I been crazy to bring us all this way, where we knew nothing, not even how to properly shop for groceries? I would never share this thought with them, because we all knew one thing: We couldn't go back.

When we were in the Philippines, our counselors assured us we would find jobs easily, but a plunge of remorse hit my gut when I heard that experienced tailors were in demand. All I could think was how much my mom wanted me to go to trade school to learn to make clothes and what a huge mistake I made by not learning the sewing business.

"But I am experienced in doing nails and hair," I told the transition team. I was shattered to hear that I'd have to go to an American school to get a license—and worse, that this could take years. Just like I'd need to earn and save money for a car, I'd need to put away a lot of money for cosmetology schooling. How insane, I thought, that I must return to school to learn how to do something I already know how to do!

Though I was utterly depressed about my work prospects here in Fort Worth, I was still grateful that Ba was looking out for us. Within the first week, he drove us to a clinic for medical checkups. We had already been through extensive health exams in Saigon and then again in the Philippines, but Ba explained that regular health checkups are essential here. What a relief it was to know Phuoc wouldn't have some strange illness no one would find until it was too late. And Ba also seemed to understand my need to find a job. He said he remembered feeling as I did, needing to be productive, needing to earn a living to buy a car and provide for the family.

After taking Trang and me and Hong's family to get green cards, Ba recommended applying to the Radisson Hotel in downtown Fort Worth, which he knew hired Vietnamese to work in housekeeping. He warned me that cleaning hotel rooms perfectly is a hard job and that I wouldn't be penalized in any way if I decided I didn't like it. He reminded me again that I didn't have to work yet, but I knew the three months of grace time would pass quickly, and I really wanted to start saving money.

Ba drove me to the hotel to apply, and I got the job. Even better, he immediately showed me how to ride the bus; he actually rode with me the first time from the bus stop near my house to the downtown stop near my job. The bus route was perfect. I liked the idea of not bothering other people to get around, not relying on anyone else for me to get to work.

Even though I had never cleaned professionally in my life, there was no way I'd have turned down this opportunity. It paid $4.25 an hour, and I was thrilled to be earning already. Trang was eager to work as well, but it took him longer to find something. Eventually, he was hired at a place manufacturing air-conditioning ducts. Now we could both save up to buy a car.

Arriving for work at the hotel on my first day, I was terrified. I didn't know the first thing about cleaning rooms. I didn't know what was expected of me or what to do if a guest asked me for something. Thank God, there were angels looking out for me—in the form of three Vietnamese coworkers.

"Don't worry! We know what you're going through," said Be, one of the three women who would become my lifelong friends. The trio had been at the hotel for almost two years. "We were new at this, too."

Be, Huong, and Hung stuck to me like glue for three days. It was a whirlwind of lessons: They taught me to make beds in the American custom, clean bathrooms, and knock out the checklist to make sure everything—especially the large bathroom mirror—was shining clean. Their expertise was such that each one of them could clean a guest room and its bathroom in less than one hour. I couldn't imagine ever doing that so quickly.

But within just a few days, the supervisor said I was ready for my own cart. I was stunned but excited. First she assigned me eight rooms, but I wasn't quick yet. Panic set in the first day when I realized I couldn't complete my eight rooms within my eight-hour shift. I tore down the hall, looking for help. I saw the cart belonging to Hung and burst into the room where she was cleaning.

"I'm going to lose my job! What should I do?" I asked, my hands flying around.

"Hold on, take a breath," Hung said with a calm smile. She patted my hands. "We will help you."

And within minutes, all three of my new friends helped me complete the two rooms I had left before my shift ended. It was one of those days when I knew God was watching out for me.

My pace picked up quickly. Soon, I had my eight rooms handled in time. Once Katie, the supervisor, saw how rapidly I caught on, she gave me twelve rooms. Within a few weeks, I was given sixteen rooms to clean in one eight-hour shift. It felt so good to be appreciated and to know I was performing well.

Perhaps best of all was having friendship back in my life again. The camaraderie I shared with Be, Huong, and Hung helped give me a sense of belonging. Even if all I knew was the bus route between my home and the hotel, my life was moving toward a point of feeling less strange. Because of their good friendship, I found myself able to laugh—even when the jokes were at my own expense.

"Look at those legs of yours!" Huong said one day when we chatted during a break. "You're a hairy girl, aren't you?"

I looked past the hem of my maroon uniform, examining myself from my knees to my ankles. They looked fine to me.

"What are you talking about? My legs are okay," I said defensively.

"Chica, you really don't shave, do you?" said Maria, a Mexican American woman who worked with us and helped us with our English. "All women shave their legs in America."

This was shocking to me. We didn't do that in Vietnam! In our culture we shaved our faces but not our legs. But Maria and my Vietnamese friends convinced me that if I wanted to be more American, I'd better get with the program. So one night, I went home and shaved, but I used Chaun's old razor, and it gave me terrible razor burn. To try to soothe my skin, I slathered on some kind of lotion that only stung and burned it worse. I was convinced they were playing a joke on me.

The next day, I arrived at work and accused them of tricking me. I showed them my legs, still splotchy from razor burn and irritating lotion, and they just burst into laughter.

"Girl, you have much to learn," Hung said. "But we will teach you."

I realized they meant well, and I had to laugh with them about my own cluelessness. I knew that though I had a big learning curve, I had experts to guide me.

Going to work became such a pleasure, largely because of the guests. Whereas I'd been so scared that my lack of familiarity and language would make me a subject of scorn, I found the overwhelming majority of hotel patrons to be kind and patient. People were generally eager to help and would give me a chance to get it right if I didn't understand something right away. I loved that about this new culture, one where people were so willing to help each other.

While I lived in fear that I'd do something wrong and lose my job—and my wonderful new friends along with it—more often than not I stumbled across reminders that God was looking out for me. One came in the form of a particularly sweet guest who was still in her room when I knocked on the door to announce I was there to clean.

"Housekeeping," I said, rapping on the door.

A middle-aged woman with short blond hair opened the door. She smiled and said, pointing to the phone, "Come on in. I'm waiting for a phone call, so I'll be here for a while."

I stopped and gestured that I could return later. She shook her head and waved me in.

"You're recently arrived from Vietnam, is that right? I am so impressed that you're brave enough to find your way in this new country."

I nodded, pretty sure I understood what she was saying. The door to the room was still propped open, and Hung was passing by. She noticed us in attempted conversation and stopped in to help.

The sweet guest told Hung that she would like to say a prayer for me. Hung told me what she said, and I thought I'd cry with gratitude and relief that nothing was wrong. Hung quietly slipped out while the lady took my hands in hers, closed her eyes, and said a prayer, asking for blessings on this child of God. Me. As time went on, I remembered how this gracious stranger asked God to bless me.

Each day, however, I worried that something would interfere with my rapid progress at work. The pressure to finish quickly and perfectly was intense, and supervisors randomly checked rooms, pulling back the bedspread to be sure the sheets underneath were absolutely smooth and the corners folded expertly, the towels uniformly folded and stacked, the extra toilet paper rolls stacked in an even line, the tub gleamingly spotless with not a drop of water visible, and the mirror without even a faint streak. Even today, when I check into a hotel room, I feel such appreciation for the work a housekeeper has done to make that room look absolutely perfect.

Of course, it's complicated enormously when a guest leaves the room a terrible mess.

Though the Radisson was a nice hotel and most guests were not pigs, there were times when I'd open the door and feel a dagger of fear tear at the space between my heart and stomach. The worst days were the ones when trash was truly piled everywhere—torn fast food bags scattered about, the contents strewn across the carpet, and ketchup smeared on what seemed like every surface of the room. In some rooms, ashtrays overflowed onto the floor—yes, guests could still smoke in guest rooms then—and empty beer cans lay tipped over on the bedside table and bureau next to little pools of stale, smelly liquid. I can't bear to remember the disgusting condition in which some guests sometimes left the bathroom.

Cleaning one guest room that had been left in awful shape might take well over an hour, and that would screw up the rest of the schedule. Many days, I never took a break for lunch, even though the hotel paid for time off during lunch break and even provided our food. I thought I should just work straight through, always so afraid that I wouldn't finish my work. I never knew what awaited me behind the next door.

There were days that the food provided by the hotel was something my stomach was familiar with, and I'd sit with my friends during lunch. Everyone knew that the American food situation was still a big problem for me, which Be, Hung, and Huong found endlessly amusing.

"Sau, I get it—I got here and thought, 'What in the world are these Americans eating?'" Be said. "But you have to give it a chance. Trust me!"

"Sorry," I said, scrunching up my nose. "The look and the smell are just sickening to me. What is in that food?"

They just laughed. "It's the dairy products that get you because we never had anything like it at home," said Be. "Just take a tiny bite and see. It's chicken. You like chicken, right?"

She held out a cracker with some chicken salad she'd put on top. It looked like food that had already been chewed. That wasn't any chicken I knew. *No way*, I thought. I resisted, praying they'd leave me alone.

"I'll be sick if I eat that. I know it."

But I'd been getting so thin from working so much and eating so little that they weren't about to let me off the hook. They knew I needed the calories for strength.

Be said, "Just take one bite. If you get sick like you think you will, I will clean it up."

Finally, to get her to stop bothering me, I tasted it, and she was right. It was good, and I didn't throw up. I was shocked and relieved. Maybe this whole American food thing would be okay after all.

My progress with work was getting a little easier, though I was bone-tired at the end of each shift. Besides the brief lunch and water breaks, I was on my feet nonstop. When I'd get home, my feet ached and my upper back felt thinned out, as if I couldn't pick up even my purse without a groan. The long bus ride to and from work made the endless physical work even more tiring, and soon I found myself wanting a car.

I decided to work seven days a week, and my supervisor was happy to give me the work; she knew I needed the overtime pay. But the bus routes were radically reduced on Sunday, and the bus didn't pass my house. I could usually find a ride to work on Sunday, but I didn't like depending on anyone else.

The first Sunday I didn't have a ride to work, I stood outside my house, not finding the bus at its usual time. I had no clue what to do.

A youngish guy drove past, turned around, pulled up next to me, and said, "Are you waiting for a ride?"

"I'm waiting for the bus to go downtown," I replied, holding my hands together tightly in front of me.

"Um, I hate to tell you, but the bus doesn't come down McCart on Sunday. But I'm going downtown. I can take you," he said.

He seemed harmless, and I was very trusting. And so I got in his car. I have no idea why I thought that was a good idea, but it was fine. He dropped me at the service entrance to the hotel ten minutes later. When I told my friends at work about the nice guy, they all yelled at me! Nobody does that here, they said. People here get killed doing things like that. In Vietnam, we never worried about catching a ride from a stranger. Now, I know God was looking out for me. Again.

Working every day of the week and sharing expenses with Hong's family, we were able to save quickly. Living the frugal life I had long found comfortable, our monthly bills, including rent, were usually less than $250 for our family of four. Everything left over after bills went into savings, which grew our nest egg quickly.

Eleven

Learning English and learning to drive were high on my priority list, just underneath working hard, paying my bills on time, and buying food for the family. Why I was able to pick up English rapidly while some other Vietnamese I know—including my mother—have not is a mystery to me. Someone asked me if my ear could be more attuned to English for genetic reasons, but I don't know if that's likely or even possible. I think it has to do mostly with my eagerness to learn and achieve.

That being said, learning English was not easy at all for someone who grew up in a different language family. One of the first hurdles I had to leap was the length of English words—on average, they're longer, and in Vietnamese, most words are mercifully short. And the order in which words fall is different in English than in Vietnamese. For example, you say "old dog" in English, but in Vietnamese, you would say "dog old." But the hardest part of the language for me were the verbs. Past perfect, future perfect, present progressive, the subjunctive mood, and the list of frustrations goes on. We don't conjugate verbs as a rule in Vietnamese, and the changing tenses in English made me want to throw my English dictionary down the garbage disposal.

Instead of doing that, I learned. I tuned into the differences in sounds, tones, and inflections, listening for all the different ways a sentence can sound. Vietnamese tones are very different from English tones, as are the inflections, varying between the start or middle or end of a sentence. When asking questions in English, you place words like who, what, where, and how at the beginning of the sentence, but in Vietnamese we place those words at the end. There were many times that I wanted to ask someone where the bathroom was, but in my head I thought, *Is the bathroom where?*

Luckily, work at the hotel ended up being a kind of language school for me. There were so many of us who didn't speak English, and instead of letting us wander around in a confusion of misconjugated verbs and misplaced adjectives, the hotel management taught us. After all, telling a guest, "You need using toilet paper new," might not be the best idea, and stumbling through the King's English with the rest of the staff could result in some serious miscommunications. So every Sunday at 3:00 p.m., I'd head to the hotel basement with dozens of my coworkers to learn English. They would set up a long table with lots of the tools and items we handled in our work, and an instructor would write the names on a blackboard and repeat the words over and over. "This is a bath towel," my instructor would say, and we would have to repeat the sentence three times. We learned words for everything—soap, washcloth, water glass, and on and on.

Katie, my supervisor, encouraged me to speak English with her so that she could help with pronunciation. At first, I was hesitant to speak because I would think through what I wanted to say in Vietnamese first and translate it in my head before speaking. I welcomed any help, because I wanted to improve my usage and grammar. If I said something wrong and someone corrected me, I would remember. Katie helped me with some of my worst problems with mispronunciation, and for me, some sounds were more difficult than others: when the letter "r" is combined at the beginning of a word with other letters, as in the words "breeze" and "strong," I tend to drop the "r" slightly. At first, it was hard to get over my nervousness. But I realized I just needed to do one thing at a time, learn one thing at a time.

My sixty-five-thousand-word English dictionary was one of the few things I brought with me from Vietnam, and it was almost always in my hands or nearby. When I heard words at work, I'd write them down and, when I had a break or was home again, I'd look up the words to understand them. But despite how much vocabulary I was absorbing, I second-guessed myself constantly and wasn't always comfortable speaking. Perhaps I could have learned from television—if I ever had the time to turn it on. Finally, a good friend of mine named Alena, my first customer when I finally worked at a salon, said, "You have to try. Trust your friends to tell you what's correct." I learned a lot about the courage it takes to try something new, and how not to let the fear of making mistakes keep me from reaching my goals. I also learned that success never happens in a vacuum—successful people are always surrounded by the friends and coworkers who believe in them.

Another person who helped me with my English was our property manager, Mr. Kinley. He was a handyman who worked on both houses and cars, and I couldn't have found a more perfect person to help me accomplish the two goals I'd set out to achieve when I first arrived in Fort Worth. As an obsessive multitasker, I loved how I could work on both my goals at once, learning English through our conversations about my much-dreamed-about car.

I didn't want an expensive car, and I wanted to pay cash—no way did I want to owe money to anyone—so Mr. Kinley found a blue 1984 Ford Escort for me that cost $750. It didn't have air-conditioning, but I didn't care. The summer's heat was familiar to me, and I wasn't about to let a little sweat get between me and my dream. What scared me was the cold of winter! But Mr. Kinley assured me the car had a working heater. All I wanted was a little car that ran and got me where I needed to go, and that's what I got, with no debt strings attached.

Strangely, I bought the car even before I got my license. Mr. Kinley helped me get the little Escort in good working order, which cost me another $400, but I know I got a great deal. Then there was a significant task of getting a driver's license, which meant I had to learn to drive, right?

So my driving lessons began. One of my work friends came over to my house every Sunday and sat in the passenger seat while I drove around an empty parking lot nearby. Sometimes in the evenings after work, Mr. Kinley would come by to help me drive around that same parking lot. After lots of practice in a space that had no traffic signals, no lane lines, no roundabouts, and no other drivers, Mr. Kinley decided I was ready.

"It's time you start driving on the freeway," he said.

"What? Are you sure?" I'd been putting off the inevitable. He said he was sure.

What Mr. Kinley didn't know from observing my masterful navigation of the parking lot was that I was accustomed to the kind of driving I knew in Vietnam. That is, Vietnamese drivers go full throttle, all out, all the time. Visiting that country, you would think there are no rules of the road; it's just chaos on every street. People drive on sidewalks. Although there are traffic police in larger Vietnamese cities, they generally don't stop people for traffic offenses. Their job is usually traffic control in busy areas, not enforcing the rules that nobody bothers to follow.

And while I'd noticed people in America generally follow rules and don't habitually drive like they're competing in a road race, my homeland instincts were awfully strong when I set out for the freeway. The moment I headed onto an entrance ramp, the adrenaline kicked in. I knew this was nothing like driving in circles around the empty parking lot near my house. My survival instinct rose up with the adrenaline, and I saw the highway as a dangerous gauntlet of cars and semis through which I had to pass.

It turned out I knew two speeds—slow and Indy 500. My brain in survival mode did not understand moderation. I hit the gas, and we were flying onto the freeway. Traffic wasn't heavy because the rush hour was over, and I bolted onto the road. The cars in front of me were going way too slow, I thought.

"What are you doing? Slow down! There's no fire!" Mr. Kinley yelled, his left hand clutching the dashboard, the right hand gripping the armrest on the passenger door. I wondered if he thought it might be safer to jump out.

"Why are these people going so slow? This is a highway!" I answered.

My foot just stayed on the accelerator. Zooming was kind of fun, but kind of scary, too. I changed lanes. A lot. Without using my blinker.

"You have to use your turn signal! It's there on the steering column on your left!" he said, his voice getting frantic.

"The what? On the what?" My adrenaline-soaked brain was forgetting the English I had spent so much time learning. For all I knew, he may have been using words that were still not quite in my vocabulary. All I knew was speed.

"You're going to kill us both!" Mr. Kinley yelled as I changed lanes again, swerving to miss another car. "Take this exit! Get off now!"

That, I understood. I didn't want to make him angry because he was nice enough to help me, so I zipped off the freeway.

"Sau, drive over to that curb and stop. You're going to give me a heart attack."

I stopped the car on the access road, near a Shell station. I turned and looked at him and realized I'd really shaken him up. In fact, Mr. Kinley stared out of the windshield like someone who had just survived a near-death experience on a faulty roller coaster.

Finally, my English language skills came back just when I needed them. "I'm sorry," I said, truthfully. "I still have a lot to learn."

"Let's practice going slowly, and that means the speed limit, which is thirty-five on most streets." He pointed to a sign about 115 yards in front of us, and pointed to the thirty and the forty on the speedometer. "Think you can do that?"

After a few more weeks of safe driving, I began driving alone to work, but I stayed off the freeway. Even though I hadn't really frightened my-self at the time, I knew from Mr. Kinley's reaction that I was a menace to society on the interstate. Fortunately, McCart Avenue connects to other surface streets that put me downtown and at the hotel in fifteen minutes.

I thought I had the driving thing down, but then one morning in January, I woke up to the strangest sight I'd seen to date in the United States: We looked out the window and everything was covered in ice. We'd heard what sounded like heavy rain mixed with sticks hitting the windows all night, but none of us had ever heard of sleet. It had been coming down for almost twelve hours, and the temperature outside was in the twenties. Everything was frozen, silent.

I walked out onto the porch and nearly fell down, it was so slick. Everything was covered in white. I ran back inside and put on the warmest clothes I had over my work uniform.

"How can you drive in this, Sau?" my mother asked me.

"I don't know, but I have to do it. It's Sunday and there's no bus today. And I'm not missing work because of the cold!"

Walking in tiny, careful steps to my car, I started it up and waited at least five minutes for the heat to fill the frigid space. I put the car in gear and backed out of the driveway. No cars were coming, so I thought, *Good, I'll have the road to myself.*

I made it maybe three blocks before disaster struck. I was sitting at a red light, and when it turned green, I hit the gas. The car hesitated. Then it took off and slid into a crazy spin. I was hysterical, watching the icy world whirl around me, terrified a car would come down the street and clobber me.

None of my driving skills, in Vietnam or the United States, could prepare me for this complete lack of control. Not knowing what to do, I turned the steering wheel back and forth, slamming on the brakes, sending me whirling toward the curb on the opposite side of the street. "Oh, God, oh, God, what is happening!" I was screaming in Vietnamese, the panic obliterating any English I had ever learned. "Stop, car, stop, stop, stop!"

Finally, I took my foot off the brake and coasted to a stop, facing sideways in the middle of McCart Avenue. A car was coming from some distance but stopped before it got too close. I was crying and my heart was hammering its way into my throat. I just sat there.

Finally, I said out loud to myself, "Sau, you have to go home. Take a deep breath and drive very slowly home. You can't just leave the car here."

Of course, I said that in Vietnamese. It would be a long time before I could cope with the most stressful situations and talk them through in English.

Creeping back home and into the driveway, I said a silent prayer of thanks to God. Then I went into the house and called Katie, my supervisor.

Somehow finding my words in English, I said, "I can't drive on ice! If you have to fire me, go ahead, but I can't get there."

Katie burst out laughing and said not to worry, that nobody in Fort Worth can drive on ice and I should stay home. She assured me that my job was safe.

To this day, I don't want to drive on ice. In fact, I'd rather conjugate a ridiculously difficult verb while driving a car with no air-conditioning—in August—than put my wheels to those slick roads.

Twelve

If I believe anything with all my heart, it's that a person needs absolute focus to achieve anything he or she wants. I've always believed this. And my life in those early days, weeks, and years in our new American home was all about focus.

Sometimes, people are surprised that I was able to buy a car so quickly. The difference between me and others is that I would never have bought a *new* car then. Friends of mine who did that had big bills to pay, financing that shiny new car *for years*. I, however, lived on cash spent very carefully. Yes, I spent $750 on that car and $400 to get it running—but I paid cash. And that's how, in my first seven months, I had already saved $3,700.

I met people right away who had a lot of car and credit card debt. And while my own mother was embarrassed that I had that old beat-up car with no A/C, she was glad that its low cost meant I could keep sending money to my brother and sister. That car met my primary needs and I was perfectly happy with it. Because I am a very practical person, I gained a mentor who was like-minded. Mr. Benson, my landlord, told me he saw himself in me. He understood my drive to own things debt-free so that I could sleep better at night.

My determination won out over any issues I might have had with pride. Some friends were caught up in having things they thought gave them status, and I knew lots of people who felt that certain material possessions proved their success. Several of my Vietnamese friends seemed baffled at how I could save so much money, how I could pay cash for a car and, later, pay cash for a house. Some even asked if I was running some kind of prostitution business! I just explained it was all about focus.

In spite of my satisfaction that I was accomplishing goals and moving forward, my marriage was unhappy. Phuoc was thriving, and my mom had Hong and her family to provide the Vietnamese community and fellowship she needed, but Trang and I couldn't agree on lots of things.

Trang and I did agree that we needed a car. But just before Mr. Kinley helped me find the car I bought and fixed up, Trang came home one day from work with a car he'd bought. He never discussed this purchase with me. I happened to look out the window one evening and saw what must have been a car at one time, sitting in our driveway. This large, white, smashed-up pile of metal had simply appeared outside our house.

"Oh my—what in the world is that?" I yelled. I'd never seen such a wreck of a car before. I couldn't figure out how it possibly came to rest in our driveway.

Phuoc, who was talking by this time, looked outside to see what I meant. He turned his little round face up to me with wide eyes and said, "That's Daddy's!"

"No, that can't be. He doesn't have a car." I shook my head, looking outside and then bending down to hoist little Phuoc onto my hip. "We don't have a car."

But he was nodding his head, giving me a sweet, innocent smile. "Yes, we do! Daddy got it!"

I felt my insides freeze, and then they suddenly began to burn, and I thought my blood would boil. I put Phuoc back down and tried to keep my face calm. I didn't like to show my anger at Trang in front of our son, but I wanted to scream. Surely, Phuoc had made some mistake.

Walking into the kitchen where Trang was sitting down to a bowl of soup my mom had made, I glared at my husband. I was glad that Hong was in the other room and her family was out somewhere else. My mother saw my face and turned back to the stove.

"What's that car doing in our driveway?" I asked Trang as I sat down at the table, trying to make eye contact. He wouldn't look at me, but shrugged his shoulders. Not as in, "I don't know," but in his way of saying he didn't want to talk about it.

"Tell me you didn't bring that terrible, smashed-up mess to our house," I said, my voice beginning to rise.

He put down the spoon and pressed both of his hands flat on the table, deciding how to answer me. His thin face began to redden, and I felt a bitter taste in my mouth, realizing Phuoc was right.

Trang took a deep breath and ran his right hand through his hair in frustration. He finally exhaled and said, "We said we needed a car, and I found a good deal on this car."

It's hard to say whether I was more upset that he made an important purchase without talking to me or that he bought a horrible, mangled thing that couldn't possibly go anywhere. I asked the two difficult but obvious questions.

"How much did it cost you? And how are you going to get it functional?"

He confessed that he'd spent all of his savings. He then said he could work on it himself and get it street-legal. I was stunned.

"Okay, let's see you do that," I said, furious. I stomped out the room. For days, I would barely speak to him.

Weeks passed, and Trang worked and worked on that heap of metal. He kept taking it in for the state inspection, and each time it didn't pass. Time went on and he continued to work on it, but it never passed inspection. He spent a total of $5,000 on that piece of junk—for nothing.

It was during that time that I truly pulled away from him. I was working myself to the bone, and I felt he was going to take me down with him. Our communication had deteriorated so badly that I made a significant decision.

"Your bad decisions and your refusal to communicate honestly with me leave me no choice. You're going to leave my money to me and let me do what I need with my own finances," I told him one evening.

He just shrugged, but I knew he resented my decision. I'd wounded his pride, but I felt he'd brought it on himself. I didn't care if he was embarrassed by all of this in front of my mother and Hong's family.

The chasm between us only became deeper and wider. As I put more money away for cosmetology school, I asked Katie, my hotel supervisor, if I could wear a headset to listen to English tapes. She said that normally she would not allow headsets, but since I was so responsible and such a good employee, she'd make an exception for me. At home, I studied the cosmetology school schedule every evening. Trang refused to believe I was serious about going; whenever I talked about it, he rolled his eyes and dismissed the idea.

He couldn't understand that the housekeeping job at the hotel was just a stepping-stone; to him, it was the perfect job for his wife. Even my mom realized that the hotel job was too hard on me. From working such long hours seven days a week, I was down to ninety-three pounds. But to be honest, it wasn't the hard work or the weight loss that was a problem. In Vietnam, I worked hard, but I was the boss. I wanted to be in charge of my career, my money, my life again.

Finally, one evening after dinner, I told my mom and Trang that after two solid years of work at the hotel, I'd almost saved enough money to begin my first course. I'd be going to school part time and driving to the school after work at the hotel, where I would continue to work full time. The evening sessions lasted from 5:30 until 10:00 p.m., Monday through Thursday, and the class also met all day on Saturday. It was going to be a long haul, as I needed eighteen hundred hours of schooling to graduate. I'd be lucky to accomplish eighteen hours of school each week.

My mom knew how much I valued my ability to work in hair and nails, and she was behind me all the way. Thank God she was willing to help out even more with Phuoc than usual. Trang, on the other hand, was having none of it.

"You're not going to school," he hissed at me, narrowing his eyes. "If you keep up this talk of school, I will divorce you."

"What are you talking about?" I asked, shocked at his anger—and his suggestion of something as shameful as divorce. "You've known I wanted to do that since we got here. I'm great at doing hair and nails, and I have to go to school in order to get that job. This is happening."

He just kept shaking his head as if he didn't believe me. His voice was low and even.

"Your job at the hotel is just fine. Why do you need anything else?"

"My job at the hotel is okay, but that was never my goal. I have talent. I have skill. You know this! Why would you want to stand in my way?"

"Because I don't believe there's any school. You have men you want to see at night so you don't have to be at home with me and your family," he said, waving his arms like a crazy man.

Though I was livid at such insane accusations, I burst out laughing. All I could think was, *I'm bone-tired when I am finished at work. How in the world would I have the energy for an affair?* Psychologically, I was gearing myself up for the added challenge and physical stress of going to four and a half hours of school at night after a strenuous day of cleaning rooms at the hotel. The very idea that I could find the desire or will to carry on with men was ludicrous.

All I could do was throw my hands up in the air. "You are truly nuts," I told Trang, turning my back on him and going to put Phuoc to bed.

The same scene played out over and over in the following months as I prepared to start cosmetology school. I was focused on starting my career and was not about to let Trang's nonsense get in my way. But he was adamant that I was running around on him.

By the time I got home from school at night, it was after 10:00 p.m. Every night he met me at the door to fight with me. He was livid, positive I was seeing someone, and insisted we get divorced.

I just couldn't make sense of any of it. I was twenty-three years old, and in my culture, you're married forever. There's a lot I didn't understand about relationships, but I remember thinking, *I'm not about to let my life come to an end because this man doesn't want me.* But this thought brought up a whole new realm of emotional turmoil and conflict for me, because it is not the Vietnamese way to think. No one says, "Well, I will get out of this, start over, and find someone else someday." That simply is not done in my culture, so my only solution was to figure out how to make the best of a miserable situation.

As much as I wanted to make things better, the fights just got worse and worse. I was so exhausted from work at the hotel, the night classes, and his nightly abuse that I broke down and said to myself, "Let's get this over with."

I started by doing something unheard of in my work life: I asked for a day off. I'll never forget that exchange with Katie, and everything that followed.

At the end of my shift one Thursday afternoon, I told Katie what I needed, and she looked at me with surprise. "A day off" and "Sau" weren't words that usually occurred in the same sentence.

"Sure, Sau. But what for? Are you okay?" she asked, truly concerned.

"Well, I don't know," I told her, honestly. "My husband wants to take me to get a divorce tomorrow."

Katie looked at me as if I'd said I was flying to the moon tomorrow.

"What are you talking about?"

"That's what he says. We are fighting nonstop, and I'm sick of it. If he wants to get a divorce and will leave me alone to go to school and do what I need to do, then I think maybe this divorce is right," I said, fully realizing that she thought I'd lost my mind. Of course, I didn't know that no one gets a divorce in one day in the United States.

So the next morning, I told Trang we could go get divorced. He drove me to a police station on Belknap Street, about fifteen minutes from our house. We walked up the steps, opened the double glass doors, and proceeded to the front desk. Trang told the person working at the desk that we needed to see a policeman.

"What's this about?" the woman at the desk asked, looking curiously at us both.

"We need to get a divorce and we need to talk to a policeman," my husband told her.

The woman tilted her head to one side and thought it over. She excused herself and went inside another office. Five minutes later, she returned with a uniformed policeman, a large fiftyish man with gray hair and wire-rimmed glasses.

"Can I help you?" he asked.

"We need you to give us a divorce," Trang told him.

The policeman asked me to take a seat on a chair in the hallway while he talked to my husband. He took Trang into an office, where they talked out of my earshot for forty-five minutes. I didn't know what the policeman said to him, but my husband came out of the discussion and told me he changed his mind and didn't want a divorce anymore.

Really? I thought. I'd never felt so insignificant. *That's it? I'm supposed to just be okay with this?*

On the way home, I finally said to Trang, "What was that about?"

"The policeman said that that's not how to get divorced," Trang finally said, staring straight ahead and avoiding my eyes. "He said that getting a divorce is very difficult and expensive. He said we just need to stay married and work things out."

I felt like all the blood had drained out of my body. I couldn't believe how unimportant I felt. How am I supposed to tolerate this man, much less love him? I thought, *I'm supposed to want to work on this marriage?*

I'd made it this far, even without love, because of Phuoc, because a family unit was important. Up until that point, I reasoned that I could deal with this arranged marriage because we had a son together. And I figured I could let the marriage go on autopilot while I focused on building this life in America as a family.

But there was no way to ignore the fact any longer that we were on two different paths. We were not communicating at all. Our relationship was like the car he purchased—wrecked and useless to both of us. He had bought that car without even discussing with me what kind of car our family should have, nor how much money we should spend. He thought working myself to the bone in housekeeping was just fine. We couldn't agree on anything, and we were not moving forward. We were moving backward, and we certainly were not together in any way.

I didn't want my mother, Hong's family, Phuoc, or even the neighbors to hear us fighting, so I just kept stuffing my feelings deeper inside. I didn't want to disagree because I didn't want to fight, but a voice inside me was growing and becoming stronger every day, a voice that wanted to tell Trang exactly how little control he had over my life: *I'm going to school, and then I'm going to work, and I will eventually learn how a divorce happens, and I will divorce you.*

As I cleaned rooms every day, as I drove to cosmetology school at night, one string of thoughts kept circling through my head: *Everyone better get out of my way. I am going to school. I am learning English. And when I'm finished with school, I will ace the hundred-question test and get my license. Soon, I'll be working for myself in a salon.* I knew that once I reached that point, I could figure out the rest.

Thirteen

As if preparing for a salon career and studying English while dealing with Trang's jealousy wasn't enough stress, I decided to build another business on the side. I saved and saved, determined to see that my money made money. I saw that people in America who worked hard could achieve almost anything, and I wanted to be part of that process.

Our property manager, Mr. Benson, was a self-made millionaire who owned a lot of properties. He saw my desire to build a successful life and my willingness to work hard to do it, so he let me moonlight by cleaning his rental houses. During that time, he taught me a lot about how he updated the homes he owned, managed, and rented, and I was curious to find out how that worked. He enjoyed helping people who showed a good work ethic, and I was glad to make extra money and start learning new skills.

One day I asked Mr. Benson why he was willing to spend so much time teaching me what he knew, and he told me his story. He said that when he was younger, he had a great family, a big house, and a lot of money. Then one day his wife kicked him out, divorced him, and took everything. He ended up homeless, living under a bridge.

Because he needed to eat, he took day-labor jobs. Then some of the people who hired him as a handyman saw that he was a hard worker and gave him more responsibility. Soon he was managing properties for people. He continued to work hard and save his money, sometimes only eating one banana a day to survive, and eventually he was able to buy run-down properties for cheap that he could fix up and either sell or rent out. From these humble beginnings, he became the original house flipper.

Once he was firmly back on his feet, he remembered his time under the bridge and realized that he was now in a position to help others. He decided that he had a mission: when he crossed paths with hardworking people who were trying to help themselves, he would help them if he could.

It was clear he didn't just play lip service to this promise; as a matter of fact, his mission helped someone who not only became a close friend to Mr. Benson, but a close friend to me as well. Mr. Benson met his property manager, Mr. Kinley, for the first time at the day-labor spot where he often found workers. Mr. Kinley was homeless at the time and backpacking from California. He struck Mr. Benson as a hard worker who kept his word, so he gave Mr. Kinley a chance. Soon they became friends, and Mr. Benson took Mr. Kinley under his wing, eventually making him his property manager. As I sat there listening to his story, I felt enormous gratitude that people like Mr. Benson were willing to take a chance on someone like Mr. Kinley or on someone like me, a woman brand new to this country. The generosity of people I meet here still astounds me.

Mr. Benson and I would talk during the times I would clean houses for him.

"Sau, how many days a week do you work?"

"Seven, when I can."

"When do you go shopping?"

"I usually don't have time to go shopping except to buy food."

He then joked with me that since I had no time to spend money, I must be keeping money under my mattress. At the time I didn't realize that it was just an expression, so I was shocked that he made such a good guess. That wasn't my only hiding place, but I made a note to myself to move the mattress money since it must be an obvious place. I didn't yet understand how American banking worked—in Vietnam my family and friends didn't have access to banks. Since I'd arrived in the United States, I'd made sure to keep my cash very well hidden, or so I thought.

Knowing that I had access to cash gave him an idea, so one day in 1995, Mr. Benson drove me to a house at 2016 May Street, which wasn't far from the rental house where we still lived with Hong's family. Like our neighborhood, the houses were built mostly in the 1920s, and some were in dire need of repair. This house was about eight hundred square feet, with an off-white clapboard exterior, a small front porch, wooden floors in the living room, and two bedrooms. It had one bathroom and a small kitchen.

Mr. Benson said I could buy this house for just $5,000 cash.

"I can't buy a house. I need all my money for school," I protested. "Besides, I don't know how to fix a house."

But he was sure this was something I should do and said he'd show me how to fix it up and make it a good rental house.

I gave him $5,000, and he gave me the key. When I told my mom, she said I was stupid, but I insisted that we had to start trusting someone. My instincts have always been good, and Mr. Benson and I understood and trusted each other; we're both hard workers, and I sensed that his intentions were good. He knew how hard I worked for that money, and I didn't think he was the kind of person who would steal from me.

He taught me about deeds and titles and arranged for Mr. Kinley, who had done lots of work for him—and whom I already knew from my driving adventures—to do the plumbing, electrical, and cosmetic work on the house. Since my small paycheck was spread thin paying for food, bills, rent, and sending money to my brother and sister, I needed to figure out a way to increase the money I could put toward renovating the new house. So I made an offer to Mr. Kinley: he could live in one of the rooms in the house in exchange for renovation work, instead of paying rent for his current apartment. He agreed, and this allowed both of us to save more money than we could have otherwise.

Life got even busier at this time: I went each day from my hotel job to school at night, and then to work on the house. It was the middle of the night by the time I got home to catch a few hours of sleep, but I didn't care. I was very excited. I hadn't even finished school and I had bought my first property! I used one paycheck to buy carpet; it was an ugly color, but it was new and it was cheap. With the next paycheck, I bought paint, and then I scraped and scraped and painted and painted. I would work at the hotel for the next paycheck and buy material for cabinets. I would work for another paycheck and buy a video at Home Depot that taught me to cut and install ceramic tile. Another paycheck later, I bought a tile cutter and ceramic tile and installed that. I learned to caulk and got the bathroom in good shape. I barely had time to breathe.

In my efforts to renovate my new rental property, I was sometimes so tired that I overlooked small but important details, although usually the result was comic, not tragic. One day I worked on the kitchen, installing the thick commercial vinyl tile. I was so focused on making sure that I made the cuts right, laid the tiles in the correct pattern with the right amount of glue, and avoided leaving gaps between the tiles, that I didn't pay attention to how dirty and covered with goo I had become. It was getting late, and my back was sore and my fingers and legs were numb, so I sat down and took a little break. After several minutes I decided to get back to work and tried to get up to get more tile, but I couldn't. At the time I thought I had become so tired that I was unable to stand. *That's it*, I thought, *I've crippled myself with too much work.*

I caught my breath and gathered my energy to force myself up. And still, I couldn't budge an inch. By this time I was frustrated, and I tried to figure out what was wrong. Then it dawned on me—I had glued my butt to the floor. As I had been laying tile, I kept wiping the excess glue on my pants, and when I sat down to rest, the glue had time to set, pasting my butt to the brand new tile! After several minutes of laughing and then several more wiggling on the floor, I finally was able to free myself.

And then one day it was finished. My own property! With new paint and carpet and tile! Considering the sweat and patience it took to make it through those months, as well as the fact that I had used up all of my savings, I felt as if I had just won a gold medal in the Olympics.

As part of our agreement, since he had worked for free, Mr. Kinley was able to stay in the house as long as he would help me fix whatever came up. I had additional plans for the other bedroom, as my life was taking a momentous turn by this time.

My marriage had been hanging on by the thinnest imaginable thread. I was building my finances and finding new directions for success and independence. Trang had not been in the least bit supportive of any of my goals or the work I put into making them into realities.

It was never my habit to dump my problems on my friends at the hotel, and I didn't want to share my personal woes with new friends I was making at school. Unfortunately, my mother didn't understand my complete disconnection with my husband. If I wanted to figure out my life, I had to do it myself, and so I spent a lot of time sorting it all out in my head.

As I drove to work at the hotel in the morning, as I cleaned sixteen rooms each day at the hotel, as I drove to school at night, and as I scraped and painted and laid tile, I thought it all through.

"I can't fight with Trang anymore, and I can't live with this day-in, day-out resentment we feel toward each other," I said to myself. "Our marriage is one big lie, and it's always been that way. He wants a simple do-nothing wife that I can never be. I want a husband who believes in me and is proud of my accomplishments, and he will never be that. We don't love each other. We don't even like each other. This has to end."

And that's what I said to the lawyer I found in a small one-story building made of rose-colored brick on Berry Street. I filled out some papers, paid the lawyer some money, and Trang was served with his papers a few days later. He talked to me less than ever, but I don't think he was surprised or upset. Because I was the one instigating the divorce, he got to blame me, and maybe that's what he needed to move on. Maybe he was even relieved. I know I was.

Even though Trang and I were barely speaking to one another, I had to make one thing clear: I wanted him to see Phuoc as much as he saw fit. The last thing I ever wanted was for my son to go through the pain of not having a father around. Even though the judge had said that Trang could only see Scott every other weekend, since Trang worked at night I told him that he could come by anytime during the day to see Phuoc.

With that, I left Trang, who still lived with Hong and her family, while my mom, Phuoc, and I moved into the other bedroom at my new house on May Street, less than ten minutes from the house on McCart. We became roommates with my tenant, Mr. Kinley—a good situation for all parties.

But soon I would encounter more difficulties. Situations out of my control confronted me, testing my strength and my sense of trust.

After I had finished working on my first investment property, I'd exhausted all my savings. We were managing, and I knew I could build up another financial nest egg; I was good at it and I was focused. As long as I was able to work and had myself to rely on, I had no problems.

Just as I was completing my schoolwork and preparing to take the state exam, a health problem brought my life to a screeching halt. Never had I experienced any health issues, but one night I woke with excruciating abdominal pain. It was a nightmare—and it only got worse. I lay there in the dark, clutching my belly in agony, and thought, *I am going to die.*

As my mother didn't drive, Mr. Kinley was the most logical person to take me to the hospital. I didn't want to call 911; I knew an ambulance ride would be terribly expensive. Even though it was farther away, Mr. Kinley decided to take me to the Fort Worth Osteopathic Hospital instead of John Peter Smith (JPS) Hospital, which was close to my house. When we arrived at the ER, my blood pressure was dangerously low, and I was almost unconscious from the pain. The world became a blur of white walls, strange antiseptic smells, and echoing voices. Finally, I passed out cold.

When I woke up many hours later, I was wild with fear but awfully doped up. Still, I screamed at the nurse standing nearby me, "Don't cut me!"

She turned from the chart she was updating, her brow furrowed. "Lady, you are way too late. You were cut several hours ago. You were in terrible pain, but you're going to be okay."

I was freaked out at the idea of having been cut open. The concept was foreign and frightening to me, and I knew the expense must be outrageous. I was woozy from the anesthesia and pain medications, but the nurse could see I was distraught. She found the doctor, the one I assumed had operated on me. He assured me that surgery had been my only option.

"You were in great distress, and we were concerned at your low blood pressure and your blood work. We had to see what was going on in there," he said, gesturing toward my midsection.

"What is wrong with me?" I struggled to find the words in English.

"You had large cysts on your ovaries. This happens to many women. Usually, they are not cancerous, but they can still cause a lot of pain. We removed the cysts but had to take out one of your ovaries, where the cysts were so bad."

The doctor went on to say that pathology would tell us whether the cysts were cancerous. He also assured me I should recover easily, with time, but that I would need to take hormones "to make the remaining ovary healthy." I didn't question the logic. He was the medical professional and surely knew best, right? Several years later I would find out otherwise.

My troubles at the hospital wouldn't end there, however. While the pain from the surgery should have been easing, the very long incision that covers much of my abdomen became infected. The resulting illness was devastating to me, physically and financially. There was no cancer, thank God, but the road back to good health was uphill.

Between the surgery, dozens of visits to the doctor, and my lengthy recovery, I missed two months of work with no paycheck. Since I had used up all of my savings remodeling our new house, to cover our expenses we had to hold off on sending money to my brother and sister, and my mom had to get a job babysitting in order to buy food. Adding to the pain of infection was the exhausting worry over not being able to support my family. Torn apart by too many setbacks at once, I was sick in every sense of the word. Years later, I found out that the doctor let a medical student operate on me.

The blow to my finances was complete after I was discharged from the hospital and received the bill. I called the hospital and told the woman in the business office that there was no way that I could pay the bill all at once. She said I could pay it over time, but that I would have to pay at least $600 a month since that was the smallest amount that the hospital would agree to, based on the size of my bill.

I was stunned. "Six hundred dollars! I only make $760 a month, and that's if I work seven days a week. How can my family live on $160 a month?"

The lady said that there was nothing she could do to help me lower the monthly amount. The hospital wanted its $600 a month. I felt like they were asking me to become a slave, working endlessly for nothing more than the privilege of not dying in their emergency room.

Perhaps because the woman in the business office could hear the despair in my voice, she said, "You might be better off filing for bankruptcy."

I hung up the phone that day with a horrible decision weighing upon my heart. Could I sell my house to get the money for the hospital? When I told Mr. Kinley what I was thinking, he wisely explained that it was better for me to keep the house, that owning it would help me build my credit again. He was right, and I knew what I had to do. So I filed for Chapter Seven.

After all the success I had come to know, I felt I was signing that paperwork with my own blood, with a pen I'd dipped in my own heart. In that moment I felt like I had failed in the pursuit of my American Dream by letting myself be leveled by an illness and a few nights in a hospital. This experience made me step back and evaluate the future I'd worked so tirelessly to put together for my family. It was slipping away—my grip on that elusive notion of hope vanishing.

* * *

Mr. Kinley was nurturing about my illness, but over a period of five to six months, he shifted his manner in a way that I found alarming. He was no longer acting like a friend—he was treating me like a love interest.

At first I didn't know how to react and hoped that I was misreading him, but the clues became so consistent I could no longer ignore them. Based on where I was in life, I had no tools to handle this situation, and I couldn't even clearly communicate my feelings. I wanted to tell him that I saw him as a friend, extended family even, but that proved to be far more difficult than I expected.

He was an honest friend whom I treasured. Even if I were interested in pursuing a relationship, which I wasn't, I respected him enough that I didn't want him to be the guinea pig for kick-starting my love life. Deep down, I knew that my wounds at that time weren't just physical. They were emotional, old scars that had existed for as long as I could remember.

As much as I tried to make this clear in my broken English, he didn't seem to accept anything I said. As the days wore on, he became more and more possessive and controlling. I can only guess what he was thinking, but I got the feeling he saw himself as having the right to possess and control me because he loved me, as strange as that seems. I tried to tell him that I needed to get my feet under me, stand on my own, and find myself after the damaging marriage that I had escaped. But ultimately, my poor English skills and his overwhelming feelings were too much for any conversation to make sense.

Eventually the tension between us came to a head, and he confronted me. While I was at work he told my mom that he was moving out because I didn't want him there. When she told me this, I assumed that she misunderstood him, and I went to ask him what was going on.

"Kinley, you move out?" I asked.

He said yes, because I didn't want him there.

As uncomfortable as our situation was, I tried to explain that I wanted him to stay and be my friend, but only a good friend, not my boyfriend. I know that my inability to communicate had led him to the wrong conclusion about us, allowing him to hope for something that I could not give him. I remembered my words when I first tried to tell Mr. Kinley that I wanted him to live in the house for free in exchange for his renovation help. I wanted to tell him that he could be a part of our extended family in the way that Hong's family was, living together in a mutually supporting way. Because my English was limited, the best I could say was to ask him to live with us as a family. I put my face in my hands in despair when I realized the effect that garbled statement had on him.

There was no way I could think about a relationship. I was too busy with work and school. My heart had closed down after my divorce, and I didn't want to put Scott or myself through any more drama. I also knew I had to repair my body and my finances before I could ever enter the world of dating relationships or love. And truthfully, I was not interested in Mr. Kinley like that.

To this day, what happened between me and Mr. Kinley still hurts me dearly. He helped me during my first steps in America by speaking English with me, helping me get a car and fix it up, teaching me to drive, and showing me the skills I needed to renovate my new home. I will never forget him. The unhappiness I experienced during our final days together drove me to focus on my English even more. I take some comfort in the knowledge that I was able to provide him a place to stay without charge, allowing him to save enough money to buy a truck and build his savings so that he could be self-sufficient. But seeing the hope in his eyes die as I sat next to him and told him how I felt was both painful and mortifying.

So that was the end of our friendship. He moved out, and I was crushed by my own sense of hopelessness.

In the past I had been able to isolate myself from sadness and depression, but at this point everything was going wrong all at once: my health had turned to sickness, my savings and security had transformed into poverty and vulnerability, my independence had disappeared with my bankruptcy, and my friendship had become heartbreak. I was overwhelmed. Scott and I were sitting on our porch late one evening, and I saw an older couple walking by holding hands, and the sight of them pierced my heart. Even though Scott was only in the second grade and didn't understand the issues of adult relationships, he sensed something and said, "Mommy, I haven't seen you smile for a very long time. I don't like it when I don't see your beautiful smile."

The sound of his small voice hit me hard, and I burst into tears, but that was the moment I felt my heart awakening. I had been ignoring myself, trying to take care of my family and build some sense of security in our lives. It had taken a toll on me, taking on the world all by myself. Scott reminded me that I needed to have a life, not just for my sake, but for his sake as well.

* * * *

Within a year after I moved my family into the May Street house, I was able to reestablish a little of my financial security. Not having to pay rent every month helped, and taking on extra work, such as cleaning Mr. Benson's rental houses after the renters moved out, helped me rebuild my modest savings.

One weekend while I was cleaning one of his houses, Mr. Benson mentioned that the owner of the McCart Avenue house, where Trang and Hong's family still lived, was looking to sell it. He thought it would be a good opportunity for me to put my savings to work and build an additional source of income.

The owner wanted a $1,000 down and $300 a month over three years. I knew Trang and Hong's family paid $325 a month in rent, which would cover my monthly payment. All I would have to worry about was maintenance and taxes. The house also had a lot of sentimental value to me since it was my first home in America. As I sat there debating my decision, I realized that it was time to stop treading water and start moving forward. *I can do this!* I told myself. So I took the risk and bought it. I still own the McCart house to this day.

After a few months of being a landlord, I became more comfortable with the big bet I had just taken with my savings and was able to relax just a bit. As I got closer to paying off the McCart house, I looked around my neighborhood at dozens of run-down or abandoned houses. Then I thought about the thousands of people who were in my position, the ones who needed a decent place to live but did not have much money. Given the success I had fixing up my home and renting out the McCart house, I saw opportunities to invest all around me. This would help me build a future while at the same time creating affordable places for others to live.

After two years, I was able to save up enough to buy an abandoned triplex not far from my home on May Street. It was not livable, so I had to tear everything down to the studs and then hire people to put in new electrical and plumbing to get it up to code. After it passed inspection, I slowly finished out the rest of the inside, like I had with my current home, purchasing more materials with each paycheck. Since I had decided to rent the triplex to people who were working for a minimum wage just like I was, my main focus was making it safe and functional, not fancy. That way I could rent it out at an affordable rate and still make a profit.

After four months the triplex was ready for renters. When I set my rent, I based it on a minimum-wage budget. This allowed my tenants to live with less financial stress and to pay their rent every month. Although my strategy had me charging much less than other places in the neighborhood, I was able to rent all of the units within two days of putting up the *For Rent* sign. My tenants greatly appreciated having a safe and affordable place to live, and all of them have been good tenants. I had been blessed when I had arrived in America by having a sponsor support me for my first three months, and I wanted to help others out as well, just as I had been helped. Putting a house key into the hand of someone struggling may not seem like a world-changing act, but it felt great to pass on some of the blessings that had been given to me.

When people ask me how I've accomplished what I have with so little, I don't actually sing the Rolling Stones song, "You Can't Always Get What You Want," but I always think about it. By watching my expenses and investing wisely, I was able to own my own home and two rental properties—with four families renting from me—in a relatively short period of time. The key to carving out this kind of success is in your attitude toward material things, or how you define what is considered a bare essential—you need to have that definition match your circumstances. Early on when I had nothing, the bare essentials were survival items such as rice and vegetables, and of course I paid my bills to keep the lights on. When I was able to buy a car with cash—not credit—I bought only what I needed, not what I wanted. I kept in mind not how fabulous I would look in a new Honda, but how important it was to increase my options for earning an income by getting to school and back. At each step I avoided debt and only raised my standard of living when my financial security allowed it. And I never overlooked the chance to invest and take advantage of more opportunities. After much hard work, and after foregoing the luxuries I didn't *need*, I was able to create a strong foundation, one that let me finally give in to a few wants. The Rolling Stones got it right.

At this point in my life, I had a repeatable plan—buy, renovate, rent— that I could rely on to continue to improve my financial security. I loved this newfound sense of control, and I could finally catch my breath and not wake up every morning feeling like I had to swim upstream, always balancing life and death, always searching for a sense of direction.

Mr. Benson and I talked about my business plans, and he mentioned how proud he was of me and how I might benefit from yet another good opportunity. He always said that there are opportunities everywhere—you just have to pay attention.

He'd found a listing in the newspaper for a piece of foreclosed land in a nearby town. It was a little over forty acres, and it was up for auction. Since the real estate market had been recently hit hard and people weren't that interested in buying land, Mr. Benson expected the land to go for a bargain-basement price.

I went with Mr. Benson to see the property in Aledo, a farm community just west of Fort Worth. We drove around a big, empty patch of land that had a bunch of old rusted farm machines on it, and my stomach plummeted. How could I buy new working equipment, learn to run a farm, and make a go of it where the previous owner had lost the land to foreclosure? There was no way I would get a return on the investment. I had a working plan to buy, renovate, and rent houses, and this little patch of land in Aledo made no sense to me.

Mr. Benson was patient and tried to explain how land is always valuable. Then he told me about the possibilities and tried to explain that I could simply invest in the property and not have to run it myself.

"It's perfect land for some cows and horses," he said.

"I didn't come all the way from Vietnam to get into raising livestock!"

He explained that someone would lease the land from me for *their* cows and horses, but I was still nervous about the whole thing. He mentioned the long-term opportunities, too, like the value of the land for its potential as a housing development and how I could sell the mineral rights one day. He was trying to get me to expand my vision, telling me about mineral rights and tax breaks for ranch land, but this felt way out of my comfort zone. Even though Mr. Benson had been a trusted mentor, the one who kick-started my house renovation and rental career, I couldn't do it.

I thanked him, and as we drove back to Fort Worth, I felt I was doing the right thing, sticking with what I knew was working for me.

Looking back, I realize now that I didn't really understand what he was explaining to me. A little over ten years later, when that property was worth a few million dollars because of the natural gas production and mineral rights, as well as the housing growth in the Aledo area, I was shocked. At first I felt awful. I thought I was so good at business, but here was a perfect opportunity I had let slip through my fingers.

I still get all worked up with regret over those lost millions, but then I remind myself that everything works out for a reason. That little patch of land in Aledo taught me a valuable lesson. Expensive, but still valuable. I believed that I had made a good decision at the time, but I made that decision without really understanding what Mr. Benson was saying. From this experience, I have learned that if someone I trust is trying to explain something to me, I need to make sure that I get it, *really* get it, before I make a decision. I should have asked questions about mineral rights and tax breaks and how to make a short-term return on the property while waiting for the long-term payoff. Even though I was out of my comfort zone and scared of the risk relative to my abilities, I shouldn't have passed up the opportunity to learn from someone that I trusted. The Rolling Stones probably have a song for that one, too. I wish I'd heard it on the drive to Aledo.

In 2000, after I bought a fourplex, I now had a total of eight families renting from me. I still didn't charge very much, and my tenants were low-income people. Their situation was a lot like mine when I had arrived seven years ago. It touched my heart to see them struggling to make it; I probably set rent at a lower rate than I could have.

With a decent monthly income from my rental properties and my disastrous, loveless marriage behind me, the spirit of resentment that had filled my home was a distant memory. I'd become a successful house renovator and landlord, and my future in the salon world was looking very bright. My son was healthy and our little family was doing well. I'd never dreamed I could have the strong sense of hope that had finally come to live in my heart and soul.

Fourteen

I often think back to those days in Vietnam when our family "credit card" placed roadblocks along our path. It didn't matter how hard we worked or how much we dreamed—in the end, the communist party decided what step on the ladder we started on and how high we were allowed to climb.

When I first touched ground at the DFW Airport, I felt it in my bones—I had come home. For the first time in my life, I was able to experience what America has to offer everyone: freedom and the opportunity to pursue my dreams. I took this opportunity to heart. For the first time in my life, I had the freedom to earn a piece of happiness. But as I lay in the dark in our new house on McCart, staring at the ceiling, panic set in. The goal that had consumed me for over a year—getting to the land of the free—was gone, and I was left with one question.

What now?

During my first months here, I thought back to my time at the salon in Vietnam, when I could make people feel good about themselves. The craving for that sense of accomplishment set in, and I had my new obsession. But to do hair and nails in a salon here, I needed a state license. I knew beyond any doubt that my talent was strong and that I'd be a true success if I could just be allowed to practice my craft.

And then I remembered where I was—in the land of the free. I thought back to grade school, when I was not allowed to join in something as simple as Tai Chi lessons because of who and what I was. I can't describe how excited I was when the truth hit me—in America, no one and no government official could stop me from climbing the ladder as long as I was willing and able to take each step.

I had my new goal—my own salon. Even though it seemed far away and almost impossible at the time, I knew I would get there if I went step by step. I worked backwards. To have my own salon, I first needed to build my clientele. To build my clientele, I needed a license. To get a license, I had to pass a test. To pass the test, I had to take classes and put in a certain number of apprentice hours. To take the classes, I had to have the money to pay for the classes and I had to be able to speak and write English. To speak and write English, I first had to learn and practice. To do any of these things, I first had to have food to eat and be able to pay my bills in order to live. To have the money to take classes and to live, I first had to have a job.

So getting a job and learning English were tasks 1a and 1b.

Based on what we had been taught in the Philippines, I thought I had a good foundation in my new language. I felt ready to communicate when an American lady who was acting as sort of a Vietnamese refugee liaison from World Relief came by to visit and to see how we were doing and to see if there was anything we needed.

Oh, how wrong I was.

"Please to meet you," I said, pronouncing it just as I had learned. When she left, I said, "Please to meet you" again. Based on her expression when she left, I knew that what I had said didn't really make sense. For a moment, I felt like I did my first day in the United States, surrounded by food on the grocery store shelves with no idea how to buy anything. I still had a lot to learn.

I immediately got out my Vietnamese to English dictionary and found a few words to learn and practice so that I could speak better the next time the lady came by to visit. And a few days later, when I got the opportunity to get a job at a hotel, I jumped at it. Now I could get the cash I needed *and* learn and practice my English. I started with my vocabulary. For example, I didn't even know what a bathrobe was in any language, since I'd never owned one or even seen one. Then I worked up to a grammar primer and listened to tapes so that I could make a sentence that made sense.

As I practiced my new words—bathrobe, towel, hair dryer—while I cleaned rooms, I sometimes thought about what my life would be like if I had never left Vietnam. Since I wasn't Viet Cong, I had a better chance of seeing a falling star there than of reaching any kind of success. Day in and day out, a fire built inside me, remembering how unfair that life was, not only for me, but for everyone in Vietnam. And that fire spoke loud and clear:

You must take this opportunity and make it work. If you wait, it may not be there tomorrow.

Cleaning rooms gives you a lot of time to think, since it doesn't take much brainpower to clean a toilet or make a bed. As I polished and folded and pushed my cart, I thought a lot about one very important rule of life: Be true to yourself. Understand where you are and accept it. If there is something that you need to do and are not good at, figure out how to get better. If you can learn on your own, great. Do it. If not, ask for help. If you deny the reality of where you are in life and think that you are better than or above your true situation, you will never be willing or able to take the steps needed to raise yourself up to where you want to be. You can't have the eggs without first raising the chicken.

The people who checked into the rooms I cleaned at the Radisson I'm sure had no idea what I was thinking about as I wiped down their mirrors and emptied yesterday's trash. They had no idea who I was, but I finally did. I was on the bottom rung of the ladder, but I wasn't stuck there. I was a seed at the heart of the American Dream, and I was already growing.

* * * *

In 1996, after only three years in America, I was ready to take one of the most important steps on that ladder I had been climbing since I first arrived. It was time to get my state license.

I realize that for some Americans, being able to take a certification test allowing me to do nails and hair might seem like a small accomplishment. Talking with people who were born here, I came to understand that since they have always had a world of opportunities surrounding them, many don't often consciously think of these opportunities, just as they don't often think of the air they breathe. But for me, this certification test was my gateway, my bright and shining opportunity. Since I'd first decided on having a salon one day, the goal of passing this test had given me a sense of direction. For me, having a state license was part of making a childhood dream come true.

We'd only been in America for three years at this point, and I was going to night school, working during the day at the hotel and learning and practicing my English—all of which combined to push me up that ladder. On top of that, I was burning the midnight oil to work on my rental properties to build our nest egg, and trying to be a good mom, too. We were becoming more American as a family. Phuoc, who was beginning preschool about this time, needed a name that would be easy for his classmates and teachers to pronounce (think about how it sounds in its Vietnamese form!), so I changed his first name to Scott.

Life was busy, to say the least, but I was confident I was moving in the right direction.

The key, of course, was taking the state test—which scared the daylights out of me.

I was terribly nervous about the hundred-question written test. First, my mastery of English was still questionable, and there were no sample tests to review or take in order to practice for the real thing. Students were given a school notebook to study, which I had with me constantly. I studied every minute I had, even giving up the chance to visit and gossip with work friends at the hotel. But none of us knew which questions would be on the written exam.

Worse, our instructors at cosmetology school warned us that almost 70 percent of people taking the test fail on the first attempt. I assumed that many of those failing the test were already speaking English as a first language, so this news made me even more nervous.

When I finished my required hours at school, I prepared to travel to Austin for the test. I had no idea where Austin was. I'd never traveled outside of Fort Worth. The whole idea scared me. Would I get lost? Would I miss taking my test? So I accepted when Mr. Kinley said he would drive me there himself.

Huong, my good friend from my hotel job, came along, too. We left Fort Worth after our day shift was over at the hotel, hitting the highway in very late afternoon.

This was my first road trip in America, and we left after work during evening rush hour. There were so many lanes and cars on I-35 heading south it took my breath away. When I first moved into the McCart apartment, I was amazed at the number of cars on the street, but I-35 was a whole different level of busy: A steady, well-organized stream of cars were all speeding southward in a friendly, orderly manner. I couldn't even imagine the same scene in Vietnam, where road rules barely go beyond basic survival techniques.

Once the initial shock of this new environment wore off, I started worrying about my test again. As we got farther south, the road opened up, and on either side thousands of open acres stretched out to the horizon. Huong mentioned how beautiful the sunset was, but I was so distracted with my upcoming test that I barely noticed.

Always one to save money whenever possible, I insisted we all share one double room at our Austin hotel, where I lay awake all night long. Even as mentally and physically exhausted as I was (that was all the time, of course), I never closed my eyes.

Mr. Kinley slept soundly in the other bed, and Huong slept the night through right next to me as I stared out the window at the night-lights of Austin. My mind never quit racing, as one pair of questions swirled around endlessly: What if I don't pass? What will I do then?

Actually, I knew I could retake it after a required waiting period. But my worry was that if my English wasn't good enough, maybe it never would be. Maybe I would be pushing that cart at the Radisson forever. My desire to return to my career was feverish, and I just couldn't bear the thought of being delayed longer. I'd been in America for three years, and the wait to put my talent to good use and to feel the rewards seemed endless. I desperately needed to keep hope for my career alive.

In the morning, Mr. Kinley didn't say the right thing to reassure me.

"Sau, I meant to tell you to be sure and get a good night's sleep," he said, yawning like a well-rested man. "You've got a big day ahead, and you'll need to be sharp."

I wanted to scream. I had not slept a wink. "Thanks," I grumbled. He'd been nice enough to drive me to Austin, so I wasn't going to say anything grouchy, as much as I wanted to.

Once I was dressed in the prescribed uniform for the test—everyone had to wear black pants and a white shirt—Mr. Kinley drove us to the test building. When I entered, I found at least a hundred other people taking the exam at the same time.

First, I took the practical exam, and like everyone else there for the test, I brought a model—Huong. During the two-hour test period, I had to perform specific tasks according to strict guidelines. Instructors watched while I permed, shampooed, cut, and styled Huong's hair. I also gave her a pedicure and manicure in another timed test.

I knew that if at any time I didn't perform the steps according to specific guidelines, I could be eliminated. I heard it happening to others around me, but I was never worried that I would join them. During the time I was a student at cosmetology school, I gained even more confidence in my skills, working on customers who came to our school for bargain deals on hair salon services. There was almost always a line of people waiting for me to do their hair. Deep down I knew I would pass this part of the exam with no trouble, and the instructor assigned to me seemed pleased with my work.

But worry over the hundred-question written test had me in knots. All around me were people who grew up speaking English, listening to English, watching TV in English. They had no idea how lucky they were! As soon as the instructors moved us into a classroom, I was sweating. They handed me the test. My hands were shaking. Only one instructor was assigned to oversee the testing, and we were told we could ask up to two questions during the course of the test if we needed help understanding anything. Only two questions. What if I had more than two questions?

Once it was underway, my shaking began to calm. I was reading the questions without too much trouble. Relief poured over me as I scratched in another bubble. The conversational English I had learned was serving me well. And then my pencil stilled. I was stumped on just one question. So I raised my hand and asked the instructor for help.

She came over to me to see what I needed.

"I don't understand this question at all," I said, pointing to the one question giving me problems.

The instructor looked at the question. Then she turned to me, obviously confused.

"What don't you understand about it?"

"I don't know what this word is," I said, pointing to the word in question.

The word was "sex." She looked me in the eye. There were question marks in her eyes, ones that said, "Are you serious?"

"I don't know this word," I told her.

The question had to do with what sorts of precautions a stylist or manicurist should take in the event a client has AIDS or another sexually transmitted disease. I didn't understand what this word "sex" was. This had never come up while I was learning about bathrobes and bus routes.

The instructor nodded and thought it over. Then she said, "I can't begin to explain that to you right now. But I will help you. You haven't asked any other questions, so this is what I can do."

She pointed to two of the answers that she said were not the right choice. Because the multiple-choice answers were four options for each question, that left me with two possible answers. I had a fifty-fifty chance of guessing the right one. I took my best shot. Maybe I got it right; I still don't know for sure.

Then the test was over. I breathed a sigh of relief, because I was pretty sure I did okay. We were told we'd get our test results in the mail. I walked out of the classroom about a hundred pounds lighter and found Huong and Mr. Kinley waiting for me in the hallway. I'd done my best, and it was time to go back home.

On the drive home, I was quiet. Huong and Mr. Kinley let me have my silence; I think they knew I just needed to think it all through. I remember staring out the car window as the world sped by at seventy miles per hour, seeing farmers using machines to automatically gather and bale hay into rolls. I couldn't believe it—the luxury of finishing your work by machine. A sudden sadness hit me as I thought about how hard people in Vietnam had to work to do the same thing, harvesting and transporting crops by hand.

I fell asleep despite all the scenery, the wide-open sky, the thousands of acres. When I woke up about half of the way back, my first thought was about my results and how long I had to wait before I got them. Then the conversation about the word "sex" popped into my head.

I finally spoke up.

"Huong, do you know the word *sex*?" I asked.

Huong—who had been in the United States a few years longer than I had—just stared at me, her eyebrows raised and her eyes round in surprise.

"Uh, yes. Don't you?" she asked.

"No, that's why I am asking you! That was on the one question I totally did not know how to answer."

Huong and Mr. Kinley just fell apart, laughing. Huong did her best to explain to me the word I didn't know. I'd been so focused on work and family and saving money that little else ever entered my world of knowledge. Social issues simply were not on my radar, and I still held tight to the Vietnamese way of never, ever discussing things like sex, which was why I'd never learned the word *sex* in English. As we made our way back through the Texas landscape of gas stations and roadside diners, I realized I still had much to learn about my new country.

Back home in Fort Worth again, I returned to work at the hotel and kept fixing up my rental properties, all the while waiting anxiously for the results from Austin. Finally, after about two weeks, I drove up to our home after work, and Mr. Kinley came out of the house waving an envelope at me.

"You have a surprise waiting for you," he said, grinning at me. I think he had a good feeling about the results.

I fumbled for the handle to the car door. I got out of the car, wondering if my legs would hold up beneath me. I felt like I'd turned to noodles. The image of my long-dreamed-for salon popped into my head. Would that dream ever come true? Or would I be cleaning rooms at the Radisson until I was old and gray?

"Oh, my God. Oh, God. It's here?" I know my voice was high and squeaky, thanks to my jangling nerves.

"Yes. Open it!" he said, trying to hand me the envelope.

"No, I can't. I can't. You open it," I said. My heart felt like it would jump out of my chest with its hammering.

He tore the envelope open and started reading it. In two seconds, he raised his face to me with a giant smile. "You passed."

I started screaming, jumping up and down on the sidewalk in front of our house. I didn't care who heard me or what kind of an idiot I looked like.

"I passed, I passed, I did it, I did it!" I yelled, over and over.

Finally, I thought, I get to do what I love to do. That enormous weight on my shoulders disappeared—finally! At that moment, I knew I could finally begin the life I came here for. And I didn't have to prove my loyalty to the Viet Cong to do it. In two weeks, the state license arrived in the mail, and I was free to find a real salon job.

That meant a tearful conversation with Katie, the hotel housekeeping supervisor. I gave her my two-week notice that I'd be finding another job—a salon job I'd been so eager to find. I had a day off the following day and told Katie I was planning to job hunt.

Katie understood, but her face was long.

"I know you've been preparing to find a job doing hair and nails. You've worked so hard. But we don't want to lose you, Sau," she said, her eyes full of worry. "You're one of the best, hardest workers I've ever had."

"You have helped me more than you know," I told her, my eyes filling with tears. "You have been so good to me for three years. I was lucky to find this job and have you as my boss."

She looked at me for a long time. I couldn't figure out exactly what she was thinking, but it seemed as if her eyes were getting wet, too. She turned away, back to some paperwork on her desk, and I left before I could start sobbing.

The next day, I went on the job search and landed a position immediately. A very nice salon in a great part of town was hiring, and they said I could start right away. I was beyond thrilled! God was looking out for me, and I was as grateful as I'd ever been in my life.

When I returned to the hotel for my next work shift, Katie stunned me with an announcement: she wanted to promote me to a supervisor position in housekeeping. As flattered as I was, I had to turn her down, and that's when we both really cried. Before I left, she honored me at a staff meeting, telling everyone how much the hotel would miss me. It was a very sweet moment—I knew then that God had sent a special angel to look after me.

As I prepared for the first day of work at a salon in the United States, I began to think more deeply about the steps I'd taken since starting out life in America. Working as a housekeeper helped me learn my communication skills and gave me the chance to work as much as I wanted and to save money. Plus, I made friends like Huong, who are still in my world today. And though I'd been so thoroughly frustrated by having to go through long, hard hours of school to get an education in something I already knew how to do very well, God set me on that path for a very good reason. If I was just handed a license, I might have settled myself into a local Vietnamese community—it would have been the easiest path. I probably would have mainly spoken Vietnamese, had Vietnamese customers, gone to Vietnamese-owned stores, and interacted mainly with other Vietnamese people. Comfortable and easy—that's what the experience would have been. But I would have been a Vietnamese-American, not truly an American.

In order to reach my goal of helping people feel beautiful and good about themselves, I had to go through the process, as many others have, to get licensed to work in the Western salon business. This forced me to learn English, which meant I could not allow myself to get trapped by the "Little Vietnam" mind-set. I had to engage with Americans and America itself, exposing myself not only to the language of my new country, but also to its customs and culture. Some people come to America and then never leave their tiny communities, becoming stuck inside a comfortable bubble called Chinatown or Little Vietnam. Going to school and then leaving my bubble to travel to Austin really helped me feel more connected to the American way of doing things. To achieve your goals you have to be ready to work and have a positive attitude, but you also have to leave your comfort zone.

License in hand, I paused on my path to the American Dream to take my own pulse, see what I had become. That seed was growing inside me, I could feel it. And it wasn't just because I had become more a part of the culture that I wanted to join. It was more than that. It was hope, that tiny flame that I'd been nursing, the one my sister had given me so long ago before she left this world. Hope was out of the shadows now and standing in a blaze of light.

Fifteen

Opening the door to work in my area of expertise was an answered prayer. And I thanked God in heaven that my mom, Scott, and I had a safe place to live and food to eat.

Shortly afterward, another trauma—another threat to my sense of trust—found its way into my life. And I never saw this one coming, either.

On the way to the Philippines and then to America, I talked to other children of American soldiers, some of whom had always known their fathers, some of whom had only recently found them. These people had someone waiting for them. Then there was me, and a few others like me. We still had no clue.

I had grown up with no father or hope of one. I lived through all of the pain and fear being fatherless had caused. Surviving on my own—building my world without him—was my only choice, but when I let myself think about it, I often wondered how finding him would impact my life. If I ever did find my father, I would hope that he was someone I could look up to and respect. I dreaded the possibility of finding my father and learning that he could be a murderer or in prison for some other heinous crime. I didn't think I had enough left in my heart at this point to pay for another charge against the credit card of life. Because of all of this, and because I really didn't have anywhere to start looking, finding my father wasn't a high priority on my list of things to do once I got to America.

A reporter for Fort Worth's daily newspaper, who was also a salon client and a friend, found the story of my immigration and settling into American life interesting, and she published an article about it. In writing about my journey to my new home in Fort Worth, she mentioned that I never knew my father and had no clue where he might live, if he was still alive.

The article ended up on the front page of the *Fort Worth Star-Telegram*. Soon after, one morning when I arrived to work at the salon, the owner greeted me at the door with stunning news. A man living in the Fort Worth area read the story in the newspaper and called the salon. He said he was my father and he wanted to meet me.

The salon owner was so excited for me and thought that this could change my life. My initial reaction was much different. I was cautious and suspicious. I wasn't even sure if I wanted to pursue this. When I was young, I dearly wanted to know my father and who he was, but as I got older and learned to survive without him, I eventually grew a scar over that wound. I learned to move on. Yes, I may be missing something from my life, but at that moment, when I heard he might be alive and wanted to see me, that dull but constant pain evaporated.

The owner said that I must meet him and that this could be one of the most important moments in my life. I thought carefully for a couple of days. In the meantime the man kept calling the salon. I decided that if I was going to pursue this, I would need to be careful. I had to make sure that he was the real deal. I no longer needed a father just to have a father, and that meant I could approach this whole thing with logic rather than desperation.

I set two ground rules for myself. First, I needed to make sure that this man was truly my father, either via a blood test or some other way. Second, I needed to avoid drama, because the last thing I needed in my life was any more of that. Making this "reunion"—if I could even let myself call it that yet—go well meant that his other family members had to be okay with him meeting me. After setting these ground rules, I decided to start a conversation with this man who would be my father.

During our initial phone call, he confirmed many of the details of the past that I had already pieced together from family stories. But I didn't know if he got his information from the article or not. At the end of the call, he said that his wife would be willing to meet me first.

She came to my home on May Street, and we sat on the porch and talked. I asked how she got involved and what she thought about it. I told her I didn't want anything from him, and I didn't want to distract him from her and her family. I told her that I grew up with no father and that I was currently at peace with that.

"What does your husband do?" I asked.

"He's a banker," she said, and then she hesitated. When she continued, I could tell she wasn't happy with what she was about to say. "At the moment he's in jail."

These words punched through my heart. I sat there on the porch with her, watching the street traffic go on as normal, as if the world hadn't just experienced an earthquake of disastrous proportions. I couldn't breathe.

"He's getting out soon," she said. "If he hadn't been locked up in jail, he would have come looking for you sooner."

This was my fear coming to life, and my thoughts were spinning as she finished her story. *Is life just a joke? Do I really deserve another punishment?*

She finished her story. I said thank you and good-bye. I didn't want to continue.

Later I received a letter explaining why he was in prison and that it wasn't really his fault. His wife called me again and started to talk about my "father." I wanted to say, "Whoa, he is not my father yet, not until I can prove it." Instead of saying that, I told her that I needed him to take a blood test. She said that he would, and later he confirmed his willingness to give me the proof I needed. My bargaining chip was that I had to meet him in prison, so I agreed.

I went to the prison and made my way to the visitor area. I had only met one prisoner before, when I was a child, the one who came to my sister's shop and bought some lunch. The one who told me the government would kill me one day. I don't know what I expected that day as I waited for him, but I know that I was cautious.

As I entered the visitor area, a tall black man behind a plexiglass window stood up when he saw me. I went over to the booth and sat down, not eager to speak. He sat down, never taking his eyes away from mine. I felt no internal connection, no feeling whatsoever, and I wondered if that was a sign. I stared at him. Wasn't I supposed to feel a spark of recognition? Wouldn't you sense whether you were in the presence of someone who shared your blood? I took a deep breath. I felt no link, no joy, no certainty. I felt nothing.

"Hello," I finally said. "I guess you know I'm Sau."

"I'm so glad to finally know you. I've wanted to know you for almost thirty years," he said.

We made small talk. He asked how I liked my new job. He asked how Scott was, how my mom was. He was polite and said all the right things, but I just wanted to leave. I was starting to think of an excuse to bolt out the door when he interrupted whatever plan I was concocting.

"What's wrong? Am I making you nervous? I don't want to do that. I just hoped we could get to know each other," said this stranger who wanted to be my father.

"Look, this isn't easy. I don't know what to think. You don't know what it's been like," I said, not willing to share my sadness with someone who meant nothing to me.

"I don't know what you went through, but I am sure it was hard. I should have been there. I'm sorry. I'm here now." My "father" seemed to be trying hard to say the right things.

If I'd known the expression, "Too little, too late," I probably would have spat that out at him. All I knew was that I was angry, confused, and convinced this person was a liar. I don't know why, but I was.

"My childhood was hell, with no father around. I know there was war. I know it was impossible. Maybe I don't blame anyone, but even thinking my father exists makes me furious anyway."

He was quiet. Neither one of us knew what to say or how to act.

We sat in silence for a little while until he finally spoke again. "Let's just take this slowly. I hope when you get to know me you'll come to understand me."

"There's nothing to understand," I said, still withdrawn, my arms crossed tightly across my chest. "What's the point in doing anything now? What's done is done."

"Because I want to know you. I'd like to know your family. I want to try to make up for some of those lost years."

He talked a good line, but I wasn't convinced. I asked him some questions about when he was in Vietnam, where he and my mother worked. I asked him where he had been since 1971 and if he had come back to Vietnam, as I had heard that my father did. He was vague, which only made my suspicion grow.

"I know you have doubts and questions. But let's just see how it goes, okay?"

I couldn't believe that I just went into a prison for this. He was insisting that he was my father. In a way, he was saying, "What difference does it make if it is me or not? I *want* to be your father."

He told me he would get out in a week or two and would take the blood test then, but none of this was feeling right to me. Every part of me was filled with disbelief and distrust. Finally, I decided to do something that I had been debating in my head for weeks.

"I want you to see my mom," I said to the man behind the plexiglass. I knew that the meeting would be a difficult one for her, but I wanted to know what they would have to say to each other. My mother could tell me if this person was really my father.

"All right," he said. "I'll meet with her as soon as I'm out."

A few weeks later, after he was released, he and his wife came to my house to meet my mother. I introduced him to her.

"Mom," I said, "This man says he is my father." I knew this was a subject she had avoided for a long time, and the look on her face told me how hard this was for her. "Take a good look at him. If there is any memory in you that says this could be him, you have to tell me." I reminded myself that it had been about thirty years since she had seen my father, and I wanted her to be absolutely certain if this was that man.

We went inside and sat down at the table along with my would-be father. He looked at her expectantly, with a small smile. She simply stared at him, waiting for him to speak. He spoke to her in rusty, broken Vietnamese. They exchanged pleasantries of sorts.

She turned to me and said, "It's not him. I knew this man, but he is not your father. He was your father's roommate during the time the Americans were there."

The man looked at her and then me, eyes wide. "No, I am him. I am your father," he insisted. She kept shaking her head at him, glaring with saddened anger. She shook her head at me. She wanted him to leave, and I was just as eager.

But he wouldn't let up. He said time had clouded her memory and she had forgotten.

I wheeled around and met his eyes. "Then take a blood test. Prove it to me. I have to know for sure." I was both wound up and very tired at the same time. "I needed my father a long time ago but don't need one now. If you are going to insist, I want DNA proof."

He refused, offering an excuse that didn't make sense, but I knew it was because he was lying. Part of me wanted to believe him, because I wanted the missing piece of the puzzle to solve a mystery in my life, but my gut was sure that I wasn't related to this man.

Despite my doubts, I met with him a few times more because my mother had said he had known my dad, and I was curious to learn more. Perhaps he could provide information about my real father and give me a link to start to find him. He finally acknowledged that my mother was right, that he knew my dad fairly well back then. They had worked closely together in Vietnam. When I asked him where my father was, all he would say was that my father had become a big shot in Washington; he even hinted that my father was either a politician or someone otherwise well-known in government. I was intrigued on one hand, but also still angry that these questions were now bubbling on the surface of my life again.

Finally, the imposter said he would not do anything to put me in touch with my father. And adding insult to injury, although I could not prove it 100 percent, I believe in my heart that this liar and fraud pulled another dirty trick on me. The whole time he was trying to bulldoze me with his lies, he was trying to figure out how to benefit from knowing me. He'd read in the newspaper story that I'd done a good job of building my life, that I'd become successful in renovating and renting properties.

Soon after he came over to meet my mom, I realized that my bank statement didn't arrive that month. I called the bank and found out that my account was almost empty. What? Someone had recently requested a new ATM card and activated it, making many withdrawals and purchases. I had an ATM card, but I had never activated it. Based on this fake father's history, I knew that the timing of this fraud and the theft were too much of a coincidence.

I lost it. Part of me wanted to go to the police and press charges, but mostly, I just wanted this fake out of my life for good. Late one night he called me and I confronted him, telling him what had just happened to me and suggesting that he was the one that did it. He did not deny it, and I decided at that moment to give him an ultimatum in order to get him out of my life.

"If you go away and never contact me again," I said into the phone, my voice as cold as my heart felt at that moment, "I won't have you arrested and sent back to prison."

He agreed, and he vanished.

The infuriating and sad truth is that I think this horrible person knows who my father is. And with DNA tests today, I could probably find out who my father is or where he came from. I could probably track him down. But I've come to this conclusion: I made it this far without knowing. I became the determined, driven person I am on my own, and I'm happy with the way I've built this life I created for Scott, my mother, and me. Having my father back in my life could significantly alter our world in some negative way, and I don't want that. And honestly, it's become so much harder to trust people—and for me, that includes men who wanted to be close to me for their own reasons—that I'm better off just relying on myself to take care of my family.

So, with that sense of resolve, I abandoned any plans to track down my father. God had put generous angels in my life, guiding me away from the false glitter of a family that can never be. Instead, I relied on faith in myself and on my newfound hope—and let it lead me into the next chapter of my life.

Sixteen

Putting the disaster with my "father" behind me became a little easier when I focused on what I knew best—work. No more trusting people who didn't deserve it. No more devastating disappointments from the corners of my heart that should have just stayed asleep. Instead I threw myself into long, satisfying hours in a salon. Each day as I painted nails and styled hair until my body was exhausted, I kept my focus on the future for Scott, my mom, and me. I had no idea that hard work wouldn't be enough, even in my new land of opportunity.

I worked at two fine salons in succession. The first was run by an ambitious single mother, a vivacious woman whose work ethic had helped her build a good, healthy business. She took a chance on me, and I was deeply grateful. She saw something in me that she recognized, and I met some incredibly wonderful people at that salon. Although I was hired on to do hair and nails, soon after I started the other nail tech quit, and I became instantly very busy. Nails became my primary specialty.

I was working hard, and I was always trying to do my best to deliver on this great opportunity that had come my way. That girl who prayed for God to change her into someone else, the one who burned her own hair trying to be anyone but who she was, was a small voice in my head now. I was happy, with myself and with the world. My customers kept complimenting me on how well I was doing and how professional I was. Because of this, my boss was giving me raises every other week. I was looking forward to working there for a very long time.

Then one Friday morning I came into the salon and found my boss in tears.

"How could you do this to me?"

"Do what?"

"Take a job at another salon without letting me know."

This caught me off guard, and I stood there in shock, staring at my outraged boss. I wasn't sure whether she was talking about me or not, and for the first time in a long time, I questioned my English skills. Maybe I'd just misheard her.

"What are you talking about? I'm happy here! I haven't been talking to anyone else."

She said that the owner of another salon called her and said that I was going to start at her salon first thing Monday morning. I tried to tell her that I had no idea that she was talking about. She was too upset and refused to look at me or hear a word.

"Since you're leaving me Monday anyway, you might as well leave right now. Take only what you own, and get out."

I gathered the few items I had and went back to my car and got in, stunned that I'd just been fired. I just sat there for a while trying to figure out what just happened. Life had finally smoothed out for me. No land mines, no abject poverty, no botched surgeries, no fake fathers stealing my money. Then everything fell apart, and I hadn't done anything wrong. I sat in the car in shock. I don't really know for how long. I just lost the job I loved for something that I didn't do, and as far as I knew, for something that never even happened. I was lost. Then I started the car and made my way home to my family, wondering how I was going to support them.

After a week and a half a customer called me and said she knew who had made the call. It wasn't a mistake, or an error in communication. Someone sabotaged me, a woman I didn't even know. The longer I listened, the angrier I became.

I went to that salon intending to confront that owner and tell her she had no right to do what she did.

"Welcome Sau Le, I have been waiting for you."

From the look on her face, I knew this was Mrs. Ming, the woman my friend had told me about on the phone. From first glance, I thought she was Vietnamese, but then I realized from her accent, and the fact that she didn't speak Vietnamese to me, that she was from somewhere else in Asia.

I walked up to the desk and we stared at each other for a moment. "What you did was wrong," I said.

"Yes," she said, looking down at something she was writing in her appointment book, "I shouldn't have done it."

"Is that all you have to say?"

She then offered me a position on commission, and I couldn't believe her audacity.

"Seventy-thirty," she said, raising an eyebrow, "and you would receive the lion's share."

I stood there, looking into this snake's eyes, knocked completely off balance. My first instinct was to tell her what she could do with her job and storm out of there. But I didn't. That's the kind of thing you do if you don't have a child counting on you to put dinner on the table. It's the kind of thing you do when you don't have a mother who needs you to survive in a strange new world where she can't even speak the language. I didn't trust this woman, but I was desperate for a job. With a sinking feeling in my stomach, I accepted her offer.

At first our 70/30 split made me a lot of money. I was building a lot of new customer business, and my old boss proved to me yet again what a good person she was by giving my customers my number when they asked where I was, even though she was so upset with me. I only wished my new boss was as honest.

It wasn't long after I settled in that Mrs. Ming wasn't signing my checks. Once it happened the second time, I confronted her to find out what was going on.

"I want you to be a partner with me. We will both benefit from this arrangement."

I knew what was really going on. She had no interest in helping me be successful. She wanted more money, more than her 70/30 arrangement was producing for her. Most of all, she wanted to push her products, which a partner was required to do. As it was, I mentioned products to my customers, but I never pushed them on customers who might not need or want them.

I was polite, but I said no to the partnership. I thought that was the end of it, and that she would be happy with our relationship. Thirty percent of a lucrative business is better than a hundred percent of empty salon chairs, so I thought I had the upper hand.

After about a year, Mrs. Ming called me on my day off and told me to find a new job. "I have a new nail tech who will be handling all of your customers."

Part of me was shocked, but a little voice inside of me said, *Did you really expect a happy ending to this arrangement?*

"You can't do that," I said. "They're my customers."

"Not anymore. All your customers will be going to the new tech."

The rest of the conversation was brief, but it was clear even the customers I'd brought from my previous salon would be gone from my appointment list.

The panic I felt at having my business ripped out of my hands is hard to describe, but it followed me all the way to the salon that day. I walked to my station to pack up my things, and I made sure Mrs. Ming knew all of what I was taking so she couldn't pretend I'd stolen anything. I soon found out she called all of my customers and told them that I was no longer doing nails. Then she sweetly offered them appointment times with the new nail tech. If she wasn't above lying to my customers, she wasn't above a false accusation that could land me in a courtroom.

I made a vow to myself that day as I walked out of Mrs. Ming's salon. The next person I would work for would be me. I was going to rent a station and work for myself. No more drama! No more having my livelihood at the mercy of someone else's crazy nature! If I could rent a space for myself and make just a $100 a day, then I knew I could take care of my business and my family.

I walked across the street, into another salon, and told the owner I was looking for a place to work. The lady excused herself from her customer, found me a table, and made me feel right at home.

I called my customers and told them where I was and asked if they would see me at my new salon. They said yes, and they came. I was relieved to find out that most of my customers had told Mrs. Ming that they would wait to hear from me before they switched to anyone else.

When I finally realized that my snake boss hadn't taken everything from me, I was filled with gratitude for the clients I had grown to respect and love. I also realized something important about my chosen career. The heart of this business is not about money, or trickery, or besting your rival nail techs. It is about treating everyone you come into contact with fairly and with respect and giving your clients the best service you can, based on your ability. At the end of the day it will be up to each client to support you or not. If you are able to make your clients feel good about themselves, then they will be there for you.

I never bad-mouthed Mrs. Ming at the time. I didn't talk about her at all. What was the point?

Soon I was busy again. After a few months, I was surprised to see Mrs. Ming walk through the salon doors and march right over to my station.

"Hello, Sau Le. How would you like to work for me again?"

What a snake. Satan in the Garden had nothing on her. There was no guilt, no contrition on her face, just a matter-of-fact look that said this is the way the world works.

Despite the fact that I wanted to throw a tray of nail implements at her head, I gave her a polite answer. "No thank you. Please leave." Direct. To the point. I hoped that would be the end of it.

Mrs. Ming had the guts to come back two more times. I said "No" two more times. That is all I'm going to say on that. But there were a lot of thoughts flying through my head.

From that point on I have been my own boss, but it would not have been possible without the class and loyalty of my customers. They waited for me, they followed me, and they supported me throughout all of this turmoil, and I am very grateful and appreciate their kind hearts. They made me feel like I belong somewhere and to something. From my perspective this is one of the great things about America. It is full of kind and generous people who are willing to take others under their wings. People with whom they have no formal relationships or obligations. It comes from an honest desire to lift people up and help them do well, with no ulterior motive or expectation of payback of any kind. For me, this is at the heart of the American Dream.

* * * *

By 1999, I was working as much as I could and really saving money again. I owed nothing, paying cash for everything as I went. I didn't go shopping, and I didn't dine out in restaurants. Each time I bought and rehabbed properties for rental, I saved more. And at the same time, I was doing hair at night and on weekends for customers who would come over to our house. Any chance I had, I was working.

What I was learning then, and what I've tried to explain to anyone who would listen, is that as you start to establish yourself financially, making money starts to get easier to understand. I might have been clueless as to how Americans make a million or billion dollars, but I knew that if I started slowly and worked hard on building my finances, it wouldn't take that long to start making more and more money. And I kept thinking, I came to this country with twenty dollars, money I made doing hair during our short stay in the Philippines, and I had managed to grow that twenty dollars into real security. I knew that if I kept trying, I would be successful in America.

In order to bootstrap yourself from nothing, or little, to being relatively financially secure, even if your income is less than modest you must make the choice to put your ego aside and to live within your means. Living within your means does not mean only spending what you make, it also includes the rule to always pay yourself in order to build your savings. For example, I made the choice to live with roommates and in neighborhoods that were not the most desirable. I bought a used car with two questions in mind: Did it run? Could I pay for it with cash? I did this so that I could have enough left over to invest in something, which allowed me to make my money work for me. If you do this, eventually you will build up a safety net for emergencies and have enough savings left to take on some of your wants, if you choose—not just your needs.

This is how you bootstrap yourself to a better standard of living, and this is what I'm teaching my children to help them build their own financial foundation. It takes discipline, especially in the beginning. But if you are diligent, it will get easier and easier because you will get ahead of your expenses instead of being a slave to debt. In the end, isn't that what being an American is all about—freedom?

Seventeen

I worked around engaging, upbeat, and friendly clients, and the most out-going and caring ones among them wanted to see me find someone special. Although I was uncomfortable with the idea, they talked me into dating a little bit. Sometimes my clients wanted to introduce me to someone or even set me up on dates. I wasn't entirely convinced I needed that, but I decided it was probably a good idea to at least meet some nice people.

So I dated a little bit. I went out with some friendly, interesting men, people whose company I enjoyed and who seemed to be good and decent. I enjoyed getting to know them, but when they wanted to get serious, I eventually just had to break away. I liked companionship and wanted a really good friend I could trust, but the men in question didn't want only friendship. With my past trust issues still nagging at me, I just came to believe that love wasn't for me.

And dating in America, in and of itself, wasn't all that easy for me. Culturally, there were big differences between the dating world I was entering here and the marriage mart of Vietnam. Wrapping my head around this took a great deal of adjustment for me. In Vietnam, nobody talks about sex, ever. Never, ever. You don't learn about it until you're married. My mother gave me a basic briefing and that was it. Until my wedding night, I didn't have a clue.

During courtship in Vietnam, there is no fooling around, period. If you're not a virgin when you marry, you might as well be dead. The loss of virginity is considered a tragedy, and if your husband catches on, he can send you back home after the wedding. It doesn't matter if an accident causing you physical injury made you *technically* no a longer virgin—you're still in deep trouble.

Now, I realize how dated and backward that is, but when it's all you know, you don't have any reason to think it's different anyplace else. So when I arrived here, I was shocked at how dating worked and blindsided by how open the American culture is about sex. Some of my friends at the salon talked so casually about their sex lives—nothing seemed inappropriate to talk about here. I caught on quickly, and I tried my best not to raise my eyebrows and look shocked when someone discussed who was putting his boots under her bed, but inside I was trying to navigate an extreme psychological transition.

Most of the time, when clients fixed me up with friends, they were older men. I wasn't sure that was right for me. We seemed to have less in common, and I wasn't comfortable with feeling like "the young thing" that made them feel better about themselves. What's more, I was so independent, and a lot of men—especially older ones—don't get that, and they definitely didn't like it. Perhaps some of them even bought into the stereotype of the submissive Asian woman—boy, were they shopping in the wrong store!

Yet I wound up dating one of these blind dates for two years. Paul was more than twenty-five years older, but in spite of my misgivings, I realized I really enjoyed myself when I was out with him. He was smart, accomplished, and confident without being overbearing or arrogant. We had great conversations, and he was interested in so many different things. I was drawn to him intellectually, as much as anything else. He was great company for me; I was never bored. Some of the trust that I had lost was returning.

The relationship really moved along, but I didn't imagine a future with him. Working at the salon and at home, renovating my houses, making sure my mother was safe and healthy, and having the pleasure of watching Scott grow into a good, smart boy was everything I needed for a good life. I saw no real reason to change that.

But then Paul bought me a diamond ring, which might make a lot of women in my shoes happy and excited. I'm sure it was supposed to be a dream come true. Maybe for someone else. Not for me.

"What's this? It's so beautiful. And it's not my birthday," I said to Paul, when he presented the ring at dinner one night. I felt other people around us in the restaurant taking notice, which made me more uncomfortable than I already was. I had a sneaking suspicion this ring came with a catch.

"I want you to marry me, Sau," Paul said. "Surely you aren't surprised! We spend a lot of time together. I don't want to spend time with anyone else."

"Yes, but things are good just like they are, right?" I said, searching for some kind of escape. "I need to take care of Scott and my mom. They're my priorities."

"Marry me, Sau, and you won't have to work anymore. I will help you raise Scott. He will have everything he ever needs for now, for college. You should know that."

My heart sank. Take away my work? Did he not know me well enough to know how important work was to me? He knew I wasn't working just to live hand-to-mouth, that building my own security was part of my character—or did he? I realized he hadn't really been paying attention for the last two years.

An idea popped into my head, and I saw an easy way out.

"You know that I cannot leave my home without bringing my mother with me. She goes where I go."

I explained that in my culture, you don't leave the mother-in-law out in the cold. It is the Vietnamese way, I told him, to take care of our parents, absolutely. Paul was astonished. And he flatly refused.

Assuming I would back down on that point, Paul—who was a wealthy man—proceeded to tell me about the prenuptial agreement: it stipulated that if I didn't stay married to him for ten years, I would get nothing at the end of the marriage. If we were married more than ten years, I would get something, but his daughter would inherit the majority.

This made no sense to me, and I said so.

"If I'm married to you for eight years and you should pass away, and if I haven't been working for eight years, how will my family and I survive? We would have nothing."

Paul hadn't thought that through, or he simply didn't want to answer. We were at a standoff. I told him to keep the ring while I thought about it all.

I went home, heartbroken. I really cared for him but was deeply disappointed he wasn't the man I'd grown to care for these last two years. I didn't know what else to do, so I went down on my knees and prayed.

"God, I'm not good at this. Please take this pain off of my chest. Please show me what I must do," I prayed, tears streaming down my face.

When I awoke the next morning, I knew it just wasn't meant to be. The message from above was clear: I had the strong sense that I was meant to have a healthy relationship with no baggage, and this situation with Paul was definitely not that. I called him to tell him that.

"I'm sorry," I began. "But this isn't going to work."

"What are you talking about, Sau? This is crazy."

"Look, I mean no disrespect to American customs, but leaving my mom just feels wrong. She doesn't speak English. She doesn't drive. I need to take care of her for the rest of her life. That's just how it is."

He was furious. But he surprised me.

"Fine, fine. I think it's crazy. But here's what I'll do. I'll build a wing onto the house and your mother can live there. Are you happy now?"

I sighed. I knew it was only desperation that made him say that. He would regret it and resent me. The signs were all there—I needed to run away.

"No. I'm not happy. And you wouldn't be, either. One day, you'll see I was right."

And that was it. I moved on, and I was fine with that. I decided again that a life without dating and love was okay. But inside, I think my secret prayer was that God would send me someone healthy, someone without baggage. Little did I know that this prayer would be answered, thanks to the angels among my growing number of friends.

Eighteen

With each passing day, week, and month in our new home and new life, I witnessed the miracles that came with becoming American. I'd been so terrified when we landed at DFW, when we went on that first disaster of a grocery-shopping trip, and when I'd struggled at my new hotel job to finish one room in the hour I was allowed. Now joy and gratitude occupied every corner of my life. I couldn't believe how well we were assimilating ourselves into the culture of our new country—at least Scott and I. My mother, not quite so much.

None of this would have been possible if not for the angels who helped me along the way. One in particular was Alena, a beautiful soul who happened to be my very first client at my first salon job in Fort Worth, back when communication was still an issue for me. Little did I know that when Alena first sat in a chair across the manicure table from me, she would become one of the closest friends I could ever hope to find in my life.

Within two manicure visits, I knew Alena was a kind soul. She's the least pretentious person I've ever met. She seemed genuinely interested in my journey to Fort Worth and to this salon. Her warmth and friendliness were contagious; I eagerly awaited her next appointment. Just sitting down with her made me feel happy.

Alena must have sensed my deep desire to succeed. Understanding this was my first time to work in an American salon and realizing that I was still relatively naïve about the nuances in American culture, she took it upon herself to give me some valuable advice.

First she pushed me to speak in English and said that she and others would help to correct me as long as I was trying to make progress.

"If you never put yourself out there," she said, "you'll never make progress. You have to have the confidence to fail."

When I did start to speak more, one of the first comments that she gave me was that I needed to slow my pace to be more in line with the speed with which most Americans speak. Vietnamese people speak very fast, and I guess my accent, plus the fact that I was speaking a million miles an hour, was getting in the way of decent communication. And then she gave me some of the best advice I've ever gotten from a client, although this time it had nothing to do with the way I speak English.

"Sau," she began, her voice low enough for me to hear but not to be overheard by others in the salon. It was our third appointment together. "Do you know what gossip is?"

I thought I'd heard the word, but I wanted to be sure. My instincts told me Alena was someone I could trust. "Maybe you should explain it to me, please?"

"In a lot of salons, people like to talk about personal things to the person doing their hair or nails. I think they need someone to confide in. Sometimes, though, they talk about things that they should keep private. Sometimes they'll talk about other people, you know?"

I nodded, not looking up from the short, neat nails I was buffing on Alena's right hand. I did know. In just two or three weeks, I was hearing things I never thought anyone would talk about, like sex. But sometimes, people would tell me stories about their friends.

"Yes, I hear some crazy things. About people I don't know. Sometimes I think it's good I don't know them!"

Alena nodded, catching my eye. "That's what I mean. It might be good if you just listen but don't say anything. If you have to say something, make it something short and simple, like 'Oh, goodness,' or 'Isn't that something.'"

I nodded again, sort of understanding Alena but not really sure why she was telling me this. She must have read my mind, because she continued.

"I'm sure Fort Worth seems like a pretty big city, and it is, in some ways," Alena said. "But it's actually very small, where we live, in this area."

At the time Alena stopped there and didn't go into detail. I didn't fully understand her yet, but I trusted that she knew what she was talking about and that she had my best interest at heart, so I followed her advice on faith, not fully understanding the "why" behind it.

Knowing the nature of women together—in my salon back in Vietnam, families would sometimes talk about other families, and my friends at the hotel sometimes enjoyed a little gossip—I understood Alena's advice. What was foreign to me was the weight of her message; I didn't really know rich people yet or understand how different and complicated life could be at a certain level of society.

Eventually I would come to understand the deep truth behind the comment. In Fort Worth, everyone knows everybody. In particular, many women who come to the same salons move in the same circles, ones in which their reputation is everything. Certain secrets must remain within a family only, because if they're shared in the community, they can destroy a person's reputation.

Even though most of the women who move in these circles know this, there is something about a salon that just gets the mouth moving. The person working on your hair, or your nails, is pampering you, transforming you, and supporting you. It feels natural to spill a few secrets, the way some whisper hidden things to bartenders over a drink, or confess a longing to a doctor or nurse. Alena was teaching me the importance of honoring that relationship, and understanding what those women really needed was a confidant, not a loudspeaker.

The ability to keep a personal secret seems like a small thing, but it's the small things in life that accumulate into success. I've taken it to heart not only in my business relationships, but also in my own life. It's one of the character lessons I teach my children, and my husband knows it. I hope Scott and Sydney understand it so that they can apply what I learned from Alena to their own lives. One thing I have realized throughout the years about being mentored by successful people is that most of them are not successful because of luck, but because of the way they live, the way they conduct their businesses—and their lives.

As I drove home from work that night, Alena's words kept echoing in my brain. More powerful, however, was the impact of the affection behind her words: Someone I'd known less than a month was concerned enough about my success that she wanted to help me navigate through some very tricky waters.

I don't cry easily, but tears filled my eyes. Not only had an elegant lady who had struck me as quite intelligent and wise spoken with kindness to me, but she'd reached out in a way that gave me the hint of something I'd never really felt before—a sense of belonging. It hit me that salons in the United States are quite different from the way they are Vietnam, full of kind and generous people offering help and advice rather than shooting me looks that mark me as the enemy. I thought my heart would burst with joy as I realized that someone who could do or be anything chose to be friendly to me, the girl whose classmates threw rocks at her, the monster child who avoided people on the street out of fear that they'd ridicule her or tell her the government wanted her dead.

When I saw Alena again, I told her what I'd figured out about the salons here, and she mentioned that many of these people were religious. Their belief in God had created a giving heart, she said. She sensed that I didn't understand, so she explained everything to me.

"The important thing in a life," she said, "is that you believe that there is a higher power above us that is in control, not that you believe in any specific God or religion. He is above us and he is in control. Instead of worrying about all the parts of your life out of your control, you should pray to God for help and guidance."

This short conversation has made a huge impact on my life. It was a small seed planted in the fertile ground of my soul, and I nurtured it daily, until it has grown into one of the most important gifts that I have ever received.

To this day, Alena continues to mentor me about life and work. She always seems to know what is important for me at certain points in my life. She also has an amazing ability to understand how much I can mentally consume at any point in time, so she only gives me very specific and small bites of knowledge for me to apply, often packed into a single sentence or two. Because of the natural connection I feel with Alena, I have the faith to follow her advice with all of my heart. She's protective of me, which is why she was so uncomfortable about my relationship with Paul—she didn't want me to compromise myself in any way. Alena understood how I suffered when that match burned out, and she reaffirmed for me that trust was always an important part of any worthwhile relationship.

As weeks turned into months and years, I gradually made more friends among my clients. In fact, I can't count how many of my clients have become trusted friends. I was amazed that I could grow friendships just talking to these women across the manicure table or over the pedicure tub. They came to feel I was a friend, not just someone who did their nails. They brought me into their lives.

Yes, they like to talk to me while they sit in their chair across from me and tell me stories. Some of the stories are funny and some are crazy, but others are very personal and sometimes are matters of life and death. I've never betrayed a confidence, which is why these ladies are still my close friends.

Another of these lovely friends is Jane, who has sent me some wonderful customers from Westover Hills, the most elegant part of our city. In time, I noticed many of these ladies had one thing in common: They were all astonished to learn I had never been on vacation. And while a vacationless life was shocking and unbelievable to them, the idea of taking a vacation was absolutely and completely unthinkable to me.

Jane insisted I must be crazy. She couldn't let the vacation topic drop!

"Sau, *nobody* doesn't take a vacation. You need time off. You need family time to do something fun! Why haven't you done that with Scott?" Jane asked.

"Vacation is not a concept in Vietnam. I don't know anyone who has ever taken a vacation where I'm from. In fact, I don't know anyone who doesn't work seven days a week! In Vietnam, you go to work every day. There is not even one day off. It's all we know."

"Aren't you curious about what other places are like? Do you know how many interesting things there are to see in America? Cities like New York and Chicago and Las Vegas. Places like Washington, DC, and the Grand Canyon and the California coast! There are so many things to see. You and Scott have got to go somewhere!"

What she said sounded like fun, but I didn't know where anything was or how we'd get there. I hadn't even known how to get to Austin to take my licensing test for work in a salon! How would I plan a vacation, much less take one? It sounded impossible. Jane must have read my mind.

"Leave it to me, Sau. You and Scott are taking a great vacation," Jane said, giggling with delight.

"Jane, you are a good friend to want to plan something for me, but I'm saving money. Maybe I can take a day off and take Scott to Six Flags," I said, remembering that amusement park close to Fort Worth Scott had gone on and on about. I knew it would mean a lot to him; maybe I should think about not working just *one* Sunday.

"Sau, I told you, I'm taking care of everything," she said, her mind made up.

Before I knew it, Jane and her sweet husband had planned and paid for a trip for Scott and me. They sent us to the Hyatt Regency Hill Country Resort and Spa near San Antonio for a weekend. The resort was absolutely the most beautiful thing I had ever seen. There were more swimming pools than I could count, with a lazy river attached to a couple of the pools. Scott could get on an inner tube and float along the river, over and over. There were story times beside the fire pits and star-watching parties and the most wonderful food—all the American foods I was beginning to like! Our room at the resort was gorgeous, with a big, beautiful bathroom bigger than any I had ever seen in my life. We had a balcony overlooking the pool and a view of the Hill Country. It was heaven.

The idea that friends would be so generous blew my mind. I had never heard of people doing those kinds of things for someone else. And in my wildest imagination, I never thought I would have friends—my friends!— treating me to an extravagant vacation. Over time, I realized that I was getting to know some very unusual and special ladies, people who simply did things like that out of pure kindness, seeking out the joy they felt every time they saw someone else happy. That I would be the recipient of such generosity was hard to believe, even as it was happening—but I realized that my angels wanted me to feel at home in my new land.

While I wasn't yet at that point in my life where spending money on a lavish vacation made sense to me, a year or so after my Hill Country vacation with Scott, I did find an excuse to buy myself a reward for my hard work. When I turned thirty, I bought myself a new-to-me used Mercedes-Benz—and of course, I paid cash.

I had built up a quality clientele list and believed that a luxury-brand car would be appropriate at this point, but a new car was out of the question. I found a car I liked and negotiated with the dealer so that after tax, title, and license the total would be in the higher twenty-thousand-dollar range. When the dealer asked how I would be paying for the car, I of course answered, "In cash." On the day I went in to pick up my car I was directed into the finance office to sign the various papers, and then I was asked for the payment. At this time I still did not fully trust banks, so all of the rental income I had been collecting I had kept at home in tightly wrapped aluminum foil packages. I started to pull out of my purse a few of these packages of aluminum foil and laid them on the desk. "Here is $10,000, and this makes $20,000, and this $25,000," and so on. The man stared at me strangely and didn't say anything, so I guess that he didn't trust me. I started to open up one of the packages to show him the hundred, fifty, and twenty-dollar bills and started to count them. By the time I got to $2,000, he started to make funny sounds and looked as if he was having a seizure, so I asked if he was okay.

"Wait! Wait here while I go get someone." Then he quickly left the room. When the man returned with some other staff, I learned that they were expecting a check, which I thought was ridiculous, since I had told them I was paying in cash. Then I learned about the additional paperwork needed for paying in actual cash and got another lesson in American commerce. The men were very nice, and at the end of it all they were much more relaxed and enjoying my learning moment. I realize now that at first they must have thought I was a drug dealer or something!

Also to celebrate my thirtieth birthday, my client and friend Sarah treated me to a Las Vegas vacation with her and her husband Joshua. That was so exciting, and what an eye-opener! I could not believe the outlandish things I saw. Spending a few days seeking out fun and adventure— rather than adding numbers to my next paycheck—was so strange and wonderful to me.

This American vacation thing was starting to become pretty fun. Soon after our Las Vegas trip, which was also soon after I broke up with Paul, I took another fabulous trip with Scott. Thanks to my beautiful client and friend Tracey, Scott and I traveled to Newport Beach, California, to Tracey's West Coast home for a real summer vacation. I was thirty, and this was the third vacation of my life.

Our trip was a magical time for both of us, set against the backdrop of the Pacific Ocean, with each day and night bringing me into a stronger sense of belonging in America. We had so much fun, in fact, that Tracey and her husband insisted I let Scott stay a little longer so he could get better at surfing. They adored Scott and were insistent, so I found myself flying solo from California to DFW. And that's when and where God decided it was time for love to find a permanent home in my heart.

Waiting for my flight at Gate 8 in Orange County's John Wayne Airport, I somehow managed to drop my cell phone on the foot of a man sitting in the waiting area next to me.

"Sorry," I said, embarrassed, reaching down to pick up the phone. "That was clumsy of me."

"No problem," he answered, smiling a shy smile. "It's a little phone. Didn't hurt much."

I sort of laughed, realizing he was still looking at me. And smiling. *Uh oh*, I thought. He's going to flirt with me. But he was cute, so I didn't turn away.

"I'm Don Hudecek," he said, talking kind of quickly. "I'm going back to Dallas. I've been out here on a business trip. What about you?"

I smiled as I sized him up. He's nice, I thought, and very good-looking with his light brown hair and big, kind eyes. But so young! What am I doing letting this nice, very young man flirt with me?

"I'm Sau. I've been out here on vacation with some friends," I answered, wondering why I shouldn't find another place to sit and wait for the plane. But I stayed where I was. He was much too nice for me to be rude to him.

Don Hudecek made small talk about Southern California and the nice weather. He asked me what I thought of the beaches. I realized he was reaching for things to say, and then it hit me—even though he had gotten up the courage to flirt, he was feeling pretty nervous about it. But he was determined.

We chatted a few more minutes until the boarding call sounded through the waiting area. Once we were on the plane, we found that our assigned seats were just one row apart. In fact, mine was directly in front of Don's. I would find out later that he thought, like I did, that this was a very good sign. We talked through the gap in our seats. The plane had taken off and we had been flying for a while when Don mentioned that the two seats next to him were empty, and I should come back and sit with him. I asked if I was allowed to, and he said yes, so I moved to sit next to him and we talked all the way home. I was very much taken with the positive vibes I got from our endless discussion, but I kept waiting for that red flag.

Don would tell people later, "It was kind of odd—everything just clicked. Halfway through the flight, I got tingles." The truth was, I did, too, but I would never have admitted it then. I was just out of a doomed relationship and heading back to enjoy my "marriage" to my work. Still, I didn't want to stop talking to this sweet guy.

Two hours into the three-hour flight, and after almost nonstop talking, I figured I should probably drop the bomb. If the flirting was going to end, I might as well end it quick.

"You should probably know something about me that you may not like. I'm a divorced mom, thirty years old, with a ten-year-old son," I blurted. There, it was out. He could run for the exit, so to speak.

But this nice Don Hudecek surprised me.

"That's perfect," he declared. "I'm thirty-five!"

"Um, no way," I shot back. "You're not even twenty-five. It's not nice to lie!"

"I'm not lying! I'm serious," Don said, reaching into his back pocket. In seconds, he pulled out his wallet and produced his Texas driver's license. I looked at the date of birth in disbelief: There it was, his birthdate. He was thirty-five that very summer.

He looked like he'd just won a prize, beaming like a kid. I had to laugh at this adorable guy. I realized how funny it is that when you start talking to someone and you have no expectations, you just talk freely. After the three-hour flight, I felt as if he had become my best friend. We both left the plane, grinning like fools and walking on clouds.

When we got to baggage claim, I told him a friend was outside to pick me up. Right there, by the baggage carousel—just like the one I'd stood next to those years ago when I met our church sponsor in the middle of the night—Don Hudecek asked if he could kiss me.

I laughed. "No! That's crazy. I don't really know you."

He answered, "Okay, let's fix that. Let's go out to dinner and get to know each other. How is tomorrow?"

He wouldn't leave until I gave him my phone number. The way Don tells the story, I gave him all three of my numbers.

It was a very good sign.

Nineteen

I didn't accept for the next night, but Don was very persistent and wanted to know when we could go out on a date. I was tempted, but cautious. I didn't know anything about him. Yes, we'd talked very easily on the plane, and he seemed like a wonderful guy. But I'd learned enough in my American dating life that things aren't always as simple as they seem. Still, I'd enjoyed our conversation, so I gave in. I agreed to let him meet me at the salon and take me to dinner and a movie from there.

Though Don spent the next two weeks traveling, he was also meticulously planning that first date. He lived in Dallas but did all the proper research for a good date night in Fort Worth. He came over to the salon on a Friday evening, and we went downtown to see the movie *Legally Blonde*. He'd also made a dinner reservation at Fizzi, a downtown restaurant.

Don likes to do everything the right way, and he wanted to pull out all the stops. The restaurant was perfect and elegant, and after dinner he even took me dancing at a downtown club. We had a great time, and neither of us wanted the date to end. Finally, I told him I had to go because my first appointment at work was early in the morning. Don could not believe I worked on Saturday; that was the craziest notion to him, but it never occurred to me that I wouldn't work on a Saturday. Even though I had tasted the pleasures of a few vacations, I still wasn't ready to do something crazy like take a day off every week.

Proving himself the true romantic, Don sent me flowers that next day. And he wanted us to go out the next weekend, too. And away we went: Within three months of nonstop dating, Don was talking marriage. *Whoa*, I thought. *What's the rush?*

Yes, I was pretty crazy about him; I looked hard for those red flags and couldn't find a single one. You would think there was *something* wrong with the man, but no, after spending plenty of time together, I still thought he was the most wonderful person I'd ever met.

One evening, after we'd had dinner in a restaurant near my salon, he told me we needed to plan a future together. He wasn't on his knee proposing (yet), but he was making very clear that he wanted us to move forward together in a serious way. Still, I was leery about relationships and couldn't find a reason to get so serious, so fast. What's more, although he knew all about Scott, I hadn't told him anything about my mom and how she'd live with me permanently. I dreaded the look on his face when he learned those details, so I tried to stall him.

"I really like you—we're really having a great time. Why can't we just take this slowly?" I asked Don. "I want to take time to really know you. I need to see and hear the good and bad and everything. And you can ask me anything. You are free to ask me anything you need to, anything about my past."

Don, in his calm and sure way, had his mind made up.

"I want to know you only from the day I met you and forward. I don't care what is in your past," he said. "I'll tell you all there is to know about me, even though there's not much to tell. I've had a couple of girlfriends but nobody serious."

He emphasized that there was nothing worrisome in his history. No kids, no marriage—none of that baggage that worried me with the others. School and career had been his life; he had two college degrees and worked very hard. Being so work oriented and goal minded, of course, was just one more thing I loved about Don. But my instincts in this relationship were all about relaxing and letting us see how it played out.

Six months after we'd met and begun dating, Don continued to push for making plans for the future. He hadn't exactly proposed, but I knew he wanted to do that in a special place and time. Close to Christmas, Don said he couldn't stand waiting anymore; he wanted to take me to Hawaii and get engaged there.

That all sounded lovely, but I was determined to meet his family first. In my work, I hear so many stories about how families don't get along. In my culture, family is so very important, so when you marry someone, you marry his family. I know Americans aren't always this way, but I couldn't take chances.

"I can't go with you to Hawaii and make big future plans until I know your family," I told Don one Saturday afternoon in December. "I want to know what they are like and where you came from. And if you're going to be with me, they need to know who I am, too."

"Are you serious? They'll be thrilled. They figured I was a perpetual bachelor," Don said, laughing. "I've already told them I've met The One, and they're thinking, 'Whatever.' They will be happy to see this is for real."

So we went to Michigan, where Don grew up, to spend the holidays with Don's family. I was happy to find they were closely connected. They love being together, and they were very open and welcoming to me. It was a love fest all around. And that made my decision for me: It made me feel like God sent Don to me, because the fit was really right.

As I got to know him better, I came to understand how very conscientious Don is, and how concerned he is about my true welfare, my sense of well-being, and my happiness. This became clear when I finally got around to telling him about my mom living with me—and that she would be with me forever.

Around the holidays, I finally let him meet Scott and my mom. He had been insisting on meeting them for a long time, so I gave in and let him pick me up for a date at my home. He came inside, and we all had friendly conversation. After some small talk, we left to go to dinner, just the two of us. When we got into the car, Don turned to look at me.

"Okay. Now I'm seeing your life, your home. I see your situation, and you need to know this: I love you and everything that comes with you. That's how it is." In that moment, Don's words had given me goosebumps. The trust I had been missing for so long had finally returned, and I knew I was ready to tell him the truth and face my fear of losing him.

"You have to understand now why I had to take time to see how this would work. I needed to figure out how the cultural differences would play out. I come from a world where you take care of your parents, always," I told Don, still sitting in the car in front of my house.

I'd never have expected anyone in America to really understand it, and while I truly respect the American way of doing things, there was no question about my mother always being with me. When Don said he understood and was really okay with everything, I knew this was another of God's gifts to me. There would be no negotiating, no prenuptials, no building a wing on the house to keep my mother as far away as possible. This was Don. It was all good.

Now that I'd put all my fears to rest, it was time for us to go to Hawaii. It was another new place, another part of the country I had grown to love so much, and I was very excited. Don, being the best at planning everything, booked us into the Hyatt in Waikiki.

It would be one of those incredibly sweet times when we continued to learn a lot about each other and the world we experienced together. And we laughed a lot about everything, even small and silly things. One evening, for instance, we were in a fancy restaurant having a nice meal, enjoying a beautiful view of the ocean. Don loves to drink iced tea, and every time the waiter asked if he'd like his tea refilled, Don said, "Yes," because that's so customary at home in Texas. We didn't know it wasn't like in Texas, where your tea is simply refilled over and over. When we got the bill, we had been charged for every tea refill, and the tea was more expensive than the beautiful dinner. We still laugh about that.

Another day, we rented a car to go sightseeing all over the island of Oahu. I was completely in love with the scenery because Hawaii looks so much like my home—so lush, green, hilly, and gorgeous. We bought sugarcane from a vendor on the side of the road and drove to the beach,

Sau on a day cruise in front of Diamond Head. *Photo by Don Hudecek.*

where I chewed it, just sitting on the sand and feeling that we were in heaven.

While touring around that day, I saw a For Sale sign on beat-up mobile home on a little patch of land.

I'd learned a lot about buying property, and I couldn't stop thinking about how much I'd love just a little piece of this paradise. Here was a beat-up mobile home that I could fix up just like the other homes I had renovated in Fort Worth. It was a perfect opportunity. "Let's see how much it is," I said to Don. I was so excited!

Don's reaction was so quick I almost missed it, a tight expression that I didn't understand, followed by an eye roll. "Sure, call the number on the sign."

So I called the phone number and spoke to the real estate agent. He was easily as excited as I was.

"That is a great piece of land," he said, "and it is $1.5 million."

I thought I was going to die. And Don was really laughing by this time.

"No, no, no. I'm talking about this beat-up mobile home with the bushes grown up all over it. It is across the street from a pharmacy."

"Yes, that's the one."

This shocked me. I continued describing the location since he must not have understood which property I was talking about. Surely he was talking about a different place! But he and I were, in fact, talking about the same piece of property.

"But the mobile home is all beat up."

Sau and Don on the dinner cruise before Don proposed.
Author's collection.

"If you want, we will even remove that mobile home for you for free, but the land is $1.5 million."

Confused, I said thank you, told him I needed to talk with my fiancé, and hung up. I thought I was an expert at this sort of thing, after so many years of ferreting out amazing deals and making investments. And I knew hotels right on Waikiki Beach sold condos for much less. Then Don explained to me how little oceanfront on Oahu there was, and this property would be owned by one person, not shared with several hundred others.

So much for my perfect opportunity. After that, I decided to turn off the business part of my brain and just enjoy the island, and Don.

* * * *

Although I knew he wanted to get engaged in Hawaii, I still hadn't expected anything in particular or anything huge, although given Don's love of romantic gestures, I probably might have guessed he had made elaborate plans.

Don had made reservations for us on a sunset dinner cruise for our third evening in Hawaii. We sailed from Waikiki and went along the Oahu coastline.

After dinner we went out on the deck and stood next to the railing. Everyone around us watched the waters and squealed with delight every time the migrating whales surfaced near the boat to show off. A small band was playing music, and we were standing at the front of the boat near

Sau with her new diamond engagement ring in front of Diamond Head.
Photo by Don Hudecek.

the railing, with our little umbrella drinks, staring at miles of blue water, blue sky, and the island in the distance.

As we turned back and headed back toward Diamond Head, the sun was setting over the dark blue water, making a beautiful gold-colored sky. Two whales came up alongside the boat and swam right next to where we were standing. It was magical. I was thinking how great God was to create something so beautiful and how lucky I was to experience this. Don dropped down onto one knee and looked up at my face. I had been lost in the moment and didn't realize what he was doing.

"A diamond in front of Diamond Head. . . . Sau, will you marry me?" he said, a big smile crossing his sweet face from ear to ear. He was holding out a little black velvet-lined box with a stunning diamond ring at its center.

I could barely speak, trying not to burst into happy tears. The other guests on the cruise were all clapping and cheering for us. I choked back my tears and nodded my head. "Yes, Don, I will marry you."

Mixed in with my immense sense of joy and gratitude was a significant sense of wonder: It now seemed a lifetime ago, yet I could remember all too clearly the Sau Le whose arranged marriage in Vietnam was an overwhelmingly heartbreaking passage. I could see that earlier version of me, sobbing throughout a wedding to a man I neither chose nor loved. And right then, I saw myself finally letting go forever of that past, saying a final farewell to a young woman who survived betrayal and resentment in a broken, loveless marriage.

This exquisite, romantic moment with Don marked the point at which I knew I was evolving into a wholly healthy, happy me. The thankfulness I felt on that boat beside Diamond Head was the most powerful in all my life: I had asked God to send me someone without all the baggage, and Don was the answer to my prayers.

Twenty

The next day we decided to walk through Oahu's Chinatown, and by luck we came across a Chinese wedding shop that had several wedding outfits displayed in the window. I had fully adopted my new country and its traditions and had no intention of having a Vietnamese wedding, but I thought I would get a quick laugh at Don's expense, especially since the outfits for a Vietnamese wedding are essentially the same for both men and women.

"Look, honey, complete Chinese bride's and groom's wedding outfits. For our wedding, do you prefer the red and gold one or the blue and gold one?"

As soon as Don glanced into the window, a stricken look came over his face.

I pointed to the mannequin in the window. "That hat will look handsome on you."

He paused for a moment, about ready to say something, but I interrupted him. "Oh, look at those shoes for you. They're so cute!"

He looked down the suit to the shoes, and the look of pain changed into something else. I can't describe it, but it took all of my energy not to die laughing and to keep a serious tone in my voice.

Finally, he spoke, "I might be able to live with the blue and gold shirt."

"No, it is a dress, and the red and gold one is more traditional."

"It's a shirt. Humor me. And I might be able to live with the blue and gold shirt and pants, but would I *really* need to wear those boats on my feet?"

"Those are shoes, honey."

"No, those are boats. They look like gondolas."

"No, you must wear the complete outfit."

I wasn't sure how much longer I could hold back my laughter, but I wanted to see how much he could take before breaking. To my surprise, he didn't. Instead, he started to negotiate.

"If I have to wear the complete outfit, can we have a separate American-style ceremony that my friends and family would attend?"

The laughter that was about to break free gave way to a feeling of overwhelming love. I couldn't believe he was willing to even consider marrying me wearing something so very alien to him. Once again, I was reminded of how much he really loved me.

"Oh honey, I will not make you go through that if you do not want to. It is not that important to me. We can have an American-style wedding."

I'd never seen a man look so relieved before in my life.

Even though I could see the initial culture shock starting to hit home with Don, the way he handled the incident in front of the wedding store reminded me how seriously he took me and my desires. Every day, I was coming to respect him and treasure him even more. As we walked through the streets of Chinatown, I remembered that this wasn't the first time he'd been willing to embrace my culture over his when it came to us tying the knot.

Before we left for Oahu but after we had several discussions about possibly getting engaged, I brought up a Vietnamese wedding tradition that I actually wanted him to follow, if he was going to pop the question, that is. In Vietnam, the groom's family formally asks the bride's parents to approve the marriage. If they say no, there's no wedding. Marriage in Vietnam is more about whether the two families' wealth and position will be mutually beneficial—and whether the two families will get along, of course, since Vietnamese families spend so much time together. It is not really about the two people loving each other. I told Don that I had already been through that process and suffered for it. A long time ago, I decided to embrace the American way when it came to love. If I were ever to get married again, it would be to someone I truly loved, not to someone my mom picked.

I then told him that I wanted him to formally ask my mother for my hand in marriage. Even though I wasn't following a lot of the other Vietnamese traditions, I really wanted this one, so much so that I told him we wouldn't announce our engagement until he asked her.

"What if she says no?" Don asked, and I could see the concern on his face.

"My mother no longer controls my decision, but it's important to me that you ask her. It's a matter of respect. Do you understand?"

He did, as he always does. Even before he booked our trip for Hawaii, he asked her, and even though her blessing wasn't required, I was relieved when she agreed.

Soon after getting back from Hawaii and letting our friends and family know we were engaged, we started organizing our wedding. Don wanted to get married on his birthday, June 15, since he said he wanted to always be reminded of the gift I was to him. This was sweet, but it left us with less than five months to get everything in order.

Sau, Don, and Scott at the wedding. *Photo by Angie Olson.*

I didn't know anything about how to plan a wedding here in America, but luckily Carol, one of my customers, was a wedding planner, and she helped me get my to-do list in order. The first thing we needed to do was to reserve a place to get married and hold the reception, since places often are booked well in advance. We looked at several churches to hold the services, and we both fell in love with the Robert Carr Chapel at Texas Christian University, with its beautiful tall windows that let in a lot of bright light from the outside, and its clean and elegant design inside—all white except for the red carpet. Cindy, one of my customers, helped us secure the chapel for Saturday, June 15. We quickly found a location for the reception as well.

Since the wedding would be relatively soon, we needed to get the invitations out quickly. This seemed like an enormous task, and my friend Donna, who does the most beautiful calligraphy, told me, "Don't worry about a thing. My gift to you is to do the invitations for you. Give me the list, and I'll handle it."

She took one look at the guest list I gave her and said, "Wait a minute! What is this?"

She couldn't read one word of my chicken-scratch handwriting. We had to go through it name by name to figure out every one. We have laughed and laughed at that, because she had no idea what I had written. It's a true friend who will sit with you for hours while you spell out a guest list a letter at a time.

And the gifts and guidance kept coming. Several of my clients got together to give me a beautiful wedding shower in my customer Connie's gorgeous home. That day was one of many dreams coming true—the kind of thing that makes me want to get up and go to work every day: customers who were friends, who treated me more like family. Then both of us were surprised when, on our wedding day, Don's dad said his gift to us was to pay for the wedding, the reception, and the honeymoon.

As I prepared for my big walk down the aisle, my friend and maid of honor, Jane, and her mom explained to me an American tradition I knew nothing about.

"Something old, something new, something borrowed, something blue," Jane told me, handing me a beautiful pearl necklace and earrings and an old coin that had been passed down for several generations. "It's the way we bless the marriage with good luck." Then they explained that these were their family heirlooms. I started to choke up and cry, and my nose started to run. Jane's mom handed me a beautiful handkerchief to wipe my nose.

Soon I was walking down the aisle with my son escorting me, instead of the father I never had. I was dressed in a perfect wedding gown, wearing the gifts my friends had just shared with me, surrounded by a crowd of my friends and family who were all standing out of respect for the bride. And I was moving toward Don and the minister standing at the end of the aisle, moving away from all the things I had lost. As I took his hand, I was overcome with a joy that I never knew I could experience.

Don and I were married a year after we met and six months after the holiday trip to meet Don's family. So many blessings had come to me, by luck or hard work, but June 15, 2002, marked the day those two elements of my life came together. Without all my hard work, I never would have had the clients who sent me on that vacation where I met Don. And with-

Don and Sau's wedding party. *Photo by Angie Olson.*

The married couple leaving TCU's Robert Carr Chapel.
Photo by Angie Olson.

Sau and Don at their wedding reception. *Photo by Eileen Thurman.*

out blind luck, I would not have returned home early, nor would Don have returned home late. He would never have sat next to me at Gate 8, and then be seated only one row behind me, and with two empty seats next to him, to boot. And the result of all those lucky moments was a conversation that set both of our lives in a new direction.

But when I think about the nature of luck, I become more and more certain that something other than random chance is at work in my life. Perhaps God, looking down on me as I grieved for my sister, as I endured the rejection of my schoolmates, and as I climbed my way back up from that pit of despair, was directing me all along.

* * * *

Going just about anywhere for a honeymoon sounded great to me—except Vietnam. Even with my limited experience with travel, I knew there are hundreds of wonderful places to explore, and the last place I thought of was a country in which I had already spent two decades. But Don pointed out that although I'd sent my mom back to visit lots of times, I had never been home.

"After ten years in America," he said, "it's time to see family and friends again, and I want to be part of that."

While I liked the idea of seeing everyone at home, I didn't think life in Vietnam was well suited for an enjoyable honeymoon. Where I grew up, the concept of an intimate honeymoon doesn't exist. Don didn't realize the entire focus of our trip would be family, as in my extended family.

In Vietnam, the needs of the family always trump the individual couple's desire to be alone. To make matters worse, showing intimacy in public is taboo in Vietnam, and we would be viewed as being the worst kind of disrespectful tourists if we snuck a kiss in a temple or embraced on a beach. There would be no time for *us*. It was a trip to take some other time, not for a honeymoon.

But Don saw this as a challenge, one he intended us to take. I finally agreed, but I wanted to make sure he knew what to expect.

I told him there were no American-style toilets nor toilet paper. In the cities, the toilet was just a fancy hole in the ground that you could flush. In the country he'd have to go up a hill and squat.

"What do you use instead of toilet paper?" he asked.

"Whatever bush is handy."

"Are there bushes with soft leaves?"

"Not really."

This made him thoughtful for a bit. "Are there plants like poison ivy?"

"Yes."

The next week when I came home from work, Don was moving around the house painfully. I asked what was wrong, and he said that his legs were hurting him. I asked why, and he said that he had spent the day practicing squatting.

"Why? You know how to squat."

"Yes, but not with my pants down."

I died laughing and still do every time that memory pops up.

He didn't seem particularly daunted by the toilet dilemma, so I kept telling him how hot, humid, and miserable it is there with no air conditioning. I told him that the roads were mainly dirt, and that the beds were nowhere near as comfortable as ours. He just said that it could not be any worse than some of the camping trips he had been on. None of this put a dent in his enthusiasm. Oh well, I did my part to warn him.

When Don said he'd like us to rent a car in Vietnam to visit family and friends and have time to ourselves, I tried to explain that Vietnam is not like other countries. Renting a car is out of the question—the cost is insane. It's several times cheaper to pay someone to drive you around. What's more, I warned him, nobody wants to be on the roads with Vietnamese drivers. He didn't know me the first time I got behind a wheel and almost gave my passenger a heart attack; if he did, and if he could imagine a whole country full of lunatic drivers, he might have bought tickets to Italy or France instead.

I couldn't get him to agree to a different destination, so off we went to Vietnam, with him packing a suitcase half-full of toilet paper because I had convinced him there wasn't any over there. After almost two days of travel on and off planes, we were completely exhausted. Only then did he begin to understand my warnings. Nothing I had said, no matter how hard I had tried, could prepare him for the total culture shock he encountered about five minutes after we stepped off the plane and into the airport and sweltering heat of Ho Chi Minh City.

It was extremely hot in the room where we were waiting for our luggage, and Don asked me why there was a hole in the wall leading to the outside.

"I don't know," I told him. Although I had lived in Vietnam for a large portion of my life, I hadn't spent much time in airports.

About ten minutes later a donkey pulling a cart with luggage pulled up to the hole, and people reached through the hole to get their luggage. "You got to be sh!++!ng me!" he said.

"Be quiet!" I said under my breath. I had warned him that public outbursts were not a part of our culture, but I guess the sight of a donkey inside an airport made him forget all that.

My brother, Huy Van, picked us up and set out into traffic. Within seconds, Don was ghostly white with fear.

"Oh my God, Sau, this is insane. Don't ever let me drive here. "

"You haven't seen anything yet," I warned. The deeper you get into the city, there are bicycles, cars, buses, and construction vehicles everywhere, and the whole scene is crazy. There is no order to how anyone drives; it's just chaos. We did see a stoplight while leaving the city. It was the only one we saw during the entire trip.

We were famished, and Huy Van knew where to go for great food, but the simple task of finding a good spot in front of a restaurant is nothing like what we know in the States. In Vietnam, parking's a contact sport, and it's incredibly intimidating if you don't know what to expect. And the problem isn't other cars—it's other people—the restaurant hawkers who are willing to risk their lives in order to have your business.

As we drove along a street thick with restaurants, more than one hawker jumped out in front of Huy Van's van, trying to convince us to choose their little establishment. Each one of these human marketing missiles sent a stream of language through the windshield claiming their food was the best, and we just *had* to eat it. Everyone was competing for our attention and business.

"What's happening?" Don asked. "We could hit one of these guys! This is nuts!" At one point about six people latched onto the mirrors and doors of the van. Don was completely shocked. It was genuinely frightening to him, the aggressive way the restaurant people pull in business.

"How do we move?" he asked, gripping the armrest. "Do we just drive and run over them if they don't let go?"

"Never, then we will go to jail," I said.

"But they are the ones trying to essentially kidnap us."

"It doesn't matter. If we hurt them, it is our fault. They aren't technically stealing from us. They are just strongly suggesting that we eat at their restaurants."

When he didn't have an answer for that, I put my hand on his arm. "Don, listen to me: This is why you can never, ever go off and do your own thing. You don't know what it's like here, you don't know this world. Your dad told me to bring you home safely, and I can do that only if you will listen to me, okay?"

"Don't worry. Just don't ever leave my side," Don said, gulping as he looked out the window at what looked like savages to him. I think he was afraid to get out of the van, but I pulled him out by the hand and led him into the restaurant Huy Van had chosen.

Over the next few days, we stayed with Huy Van and his family, where Don was very excited to find out the house contained a bathroom. He rushed in to look at it and came running back to announce they had toilet paper. They didn't have an American-style toilet, but he still sounded like he'd won the lottery.

Don quickly came to understand exactly what I'd been trying to tell him about family and the Vietnamese ways. Once my family and friends saw me, they weren't about to let me out of their sight.

"In our country, you don't make a trip to visit family just because you want to make the trip. Usually you just travel to see family if someone is sick," I tried to explain to Don. "When I still lived here, my sister or brother would only come once every three years from Saigon. Casual travel does not happen."

This was a big adjustment for Don, who was accustomed to how polite everyone is in America.

"What if you need your space? Can't you tell them that?" Don asked, and I just laughed.

"No, there's no such thing here. The Vietnamese are all about being together, all day, every day, definitely in each other's space. You're going to see that this togetherness is very, very intense," I said, wondering if he could possibly be prepared for how smothering it would be for him.

My brother's home village, which was a reasonable distance from Ho Chi Minh City, had no interesting tourist attractions and probably had few white visitors, if any. As we sat in my brother's living room next to the window, several children from the village gathered to gawk at Don. To them he was a strange, exotic creature that didn't look like anyone else, and they couldn't help but stare.

Another big shock for Don was the size of our traveling party in our drive to my hometown near Hue. Crammed into a ten-year-old Hyundai van, in one of the hottest, most humid climates on earth, were Huy Van, his wife and their two small children, my sister Huong, her husband and their four children, and Huong's best friend. On the day of departure, here came a cousin who needed to visit his dying mother in Hue, plus his son. Huy had also asked along a friend of his to help him drive.

Don looked at me in astonishment as the group began to assemble. There would be a total of fifteen passengers in the van.

"Are you kidding me? Don't they know this is our honeymoon? Why is everyone riding together?" And then Don asked what seemed like a logical question. "Can't we just buy them bus tickets and see them there? Your brother and his friend could drive us in the van and we could meet them later, right?"

"No, we can't. Here, it's a way of treating people with respect to take them with us. We are saying they are included. To give them money to go their own way and not with us is very impersonal and offensive. The rude treatment would never be forgotten," I told Don, wishing he'd listened to me back home.

Our van was so overloaded that it barely moved and because of it, we couldn't run the A/C. So we drove with the windows rolled down, even though it was horribly hot and dusty. Our sweat caused the dust to stick to our skin, acting like sandpaper against the vinyl seats; the little ones were crying, and it was complete misery for a full twenty-four hours.

As we drove over a mountain at Da Nang, traffic had stopped for an eighteen-wheeler that had lost momentum and could not make it up the hill. About fifty people were trying to push it up the mountain so that it could start moving again under its own power, allowing everyone behind it to continue on their way. Don couldn't sit still. He jumped out of the van with his fancy camera to take pictures before I could stop him. Freaking out, I ran after him.

"Are you crazy? Don't you know they will take whatever you have? This is incredibly dangerous." I was actually scolding my husband. But he wanted to shoot pictures of the ocean, the mountain, whatever he could see. He kept saying, "Sau, it's fine."

"No, it's not fine! I promised your dad I would get you home in one piece, and you don't know how scary this is." I tried to tell him that in the past that there had been many people who had fallen off the cliff, but all he said was that he wasn't going to get that close to the edge.

"You don't understand; there are people that will push you over the edge just so they can take your camera."

That freaked Don out sufficiently. He started to listen to me a little more.

Later, Don would say that drive to Hue felt like a week, although it was only twenty-four hours.

The next day, we wanted to get a good meal and see a Buddhist temple. Huy Van said it was a big tourist destination and came with a stunning mountain view. While walking up to the temple, Don had taken so many pictures that he was almost out of film, but his extra rolls were packed away back in the van at the bottom of the mountain. Don wanted to buy some from a vendor on the street, but I begged him not to. I knew buying film off the street would most likely be a scam. Don assured me he knew the brand and showed me how the box was all sealed up.

"I know what I'm doing. I'm not that naïve."

He bought the film and we continued on the street. About five minutes later Don tried to reload his camera and was messing with it for several minutes. I asked him to hurry up. He said that he got screwed. The film had already been used and was fully advanced through. When we looked back the street vendor's cart was no longer there. Score one for the street vendor.

After Huy Van took Don back down to the van to get more film, we continued our trek up the mountain. Once we got to the top, we spent a long time exploring. The Buddhist temple was huge—open, airy, and decorated in red and gold. When Don saw a symbol that looked like a swastika on a nearby wall, he caught the attention of a monk and asked me to translate through Huy Van to ask the monk questions. Don's questions started off innocent enough. Why was it there? What did it mean to them? How long had the symbol been there? But then he started to ask if the monks knew what the symbol meant to other people. I stopped translating and spoke to Don in English.

"Don, listen to me. This is not a free country. You don't ask these kinds of questions. You keep your mouth shut, and you don't bring attention to yourself. If you do, the wrong people will start following us, and we do not want that to happen." I was scared, and Don saw that.

It sank in, finally. I looked in his face and saw the gears in his mind finally click into place, and he understood what I'd been telling him: We have incredible freedoms in America, and we take them for granted. It isn't like that everywhere else, and it certainly wasn't like that in Vietnam.

We had no intention of letting one dishonest street vendor and a mind-blowing realization ruin our "honeymoon," so the next day we went into Hue and visited the old imperial palace. It was just a tourist trap, but it was fun for us. We dressed up as the king and queen, sat on a replica throne, and got our pictures taken—our brief moment as royalty.

We stayed in Hue two days and one night to see the sights, and then traveled to my hometown. My town is very poor, but people have a lot of pride—in Vietnam, we make being proud a priority. Don and I stayed at a hotel so we wouldn't impose on my relatives' tiny homes, and in the mornings drove to my hometown. From ten o'clock in the morning until eight o'clock in the evening, I saw my friends and family. Essentially seeing everyone in the village, moving from family home to family home, visiting sometimes thirty minutes, sometimes longer, catching up with people, many of whom I hadn't spoken to since I had left Vietnam for America. Before we left America my mom had given me the rundown of everyone's current ailments and a list of the things they needed, so I bought them the over-the-counter medicines and things they needed that were small in size relative to their value. Some items that we may consider staples such as Tylenol or diarrhea medicine can be relatively expensive and hard to find in Vietnam. Some of the other things were too large to bring with us, so we helped out with money because the ridiculous exchange rate made it the obvious way to provide the most help. Since my mom had gathered intelligence for us prior to our trip, I knew most of what everyone needed, so many didn't need to hurt their pride by asking for help.

As we went about our visits the cultural divide Don was experiencing was making this idea of a honeymoon a dark comedy. Actions that may be perfectly acceptable in America are not always so in Vietnam, so I was constantly trying to be a bridge between the two cultures. It was wearing me out trying to keep track of what everyone was doing while translating all of Don's questions and the responses. For instance, in the Vietnamese culture, when you are offered a glass of water at someone's home, it's polite to accept it, but you don't have to drink it. Don had read warnings about what happens when you drink the water in the countryside. Seeing several animals grazing next to a well cemented this fact in his brain. At first he tried to decline a glass of water or tea when someone offered us a glass at the houses we visited, and it took the first few visits to get Don to understand that refusing the drink wasn't an option because our host would be hurt. I was thoroughly stressed out from trying not to come across as a snob while trying to get Don to behave within our customs. I would casually hold my glass while having a conversation, but this would stress Don out wondering whether or not I had forgotten his warning. This really wasn't the kind of honeymoon memories I had planned on making.

We were so busy with family and friends that we didn't eat or drink a thing all day. When it was time to make the trek back to Ho Chi Minh City—during which we'd listen to my nephew cry and whine on and off for the entire trip—Don and I decided that we'd better make something good happen.

Along the way, we passed beautiful beaches—although most who live in Vietnam do not have the opportunity to enjoy them. Most do not travel, much less take vacations, since survival is a full-time job. Visiting pretty beaches is what tourists do. Nevertheless, we decided to stop at Nha Trang Beach.

"Can we stay here a whole day and be by ourselves?" Don said, looking with longing at the quaint beach town and the gorgeous stretch of white sand where we could relax and enjoy each other's company. I was desperate to find some happy alone time with my husband, so I set out to make it work, knowing there would be hell to pay.

Telling my siblings and their families that I needed to spend quiet time with my husband for one day of our honeymoon went as I expected. With shock and hurt, they told me how terribly I'd offended them. But I did it anyway so we could swim and eat and have our alone time. The beach was beautiful, but only a few people were enjoying it.

Don commented on this. "This blows away Waikiki Beach. It's deeper with more sand, it's curved on each side so you can see the beach coastline while sitting here, and those small islands make the view more interesting. I know that this is farther away than Hawaii, but this is amazing."

"I know. Most of these people are from Australia," I said, looking around us. This brought to Don's attention that the people on the beach were mainly Caucasian, which was in contrast to our trip so far.

"See?" I said, nodding to the groups of pale people enjoying the sand and surf. "Vietnamese people don't take vacations."

Don even suggested we stay in one hotel and my family in another, so we could have privacy. I said okay, but I warned him that once our hotel owner figured out where Don was from, we'd get hit with the "American surcharge." At that point, Don was past caring about things like fairness or inconvenience—he just wanted a night with me without all my relatives and friends a stone's throw away. Then the hotel owner told us he needed to charge us extra for protection. Then he came up with another additional charge. And so they kept piling it on. Yet when my brother rented a similar room nearby, it was for hundreds of dollars less.

After we left Nha Trang, there was time to stop at Da Lat, a beautiful mountain city. Da Lat looks out of place in Vietnam because many of the buildings have a French influence from the time they were in control of the country. The weather is consistently cool because of its southern location and high elevation. Strolling the streets, we window-shopped and enjoyed the break from the heat. We stopped at several locations to enjoy beautiful landscapes and amazing views out into the valleys below.

We came across a shop that displayed several bottles in its window.

"Here," Huy Van said to Don, holding out a bottle of wine to him in the shop. "You'll love this. Buy it!"

As I was trying to interpret for Don, I looked more closely at the bottle. There was a snake in the wine. "No way, you're not doing this to my husband," I told Huy Van, rolling my eyes.

Don asked, "Is this a venomous snake?"

"Yes."

"Why do they put a snake in the wine? Is it just a big version of the worm in mescal, or was it supposed to have some purpose?"

"People often drink it because they believe it gives them energy and increases their virility."

Don leaned toward me and raised his eyebrows. "Does it really?"

"People say it does, but you can't drink too much at a time or you can have a negative reaction."

Don put it back on the shelf.

We did end up buying a bottle of wine with a gecko, sea horses, and ginseng, which seemed much safer than drinking snake venom. (When we were back home, Don decided not to open that bottle, and we kept it for a conversation piece. Eventually we would give it to Scott when he turned twenty-one. He loved it and so did his college friends.)

Then my brother wanted to steer Don into a restaurant where the menu includes dog and cat, among other proteins in the dishes. Huy Van thought it would be funny to see if Don could tell what he was eating. I quickly shut this down. By that time on my honeymoon, I had already been forced to act as Don's designated safety inspector, fraud-prevention adviser, and cultural attaché. Culinary gatekeeper was just one job too many for a girl on her honeymoon.

* * * *

At the beginning of our trip Don had been shocked—and somewhat concerned—that Huy Van had a refrigerator, but didn't have it plugged in. "Don't they know that it needs to be plugged in to keep things cold and fresh?" I tried to explain that it's not necessary, that people go to the store every day to buy fresh food. For most people the electricity is too expensive to keep a refrigerator running, so most use them mainly to keep the flies off the food. Later, when my sister-in-law was preparing a chicken for a meal in our honor, she took the chicken out back to butcher. This was nothing strange to Don, since he had raised chickens when he was younger, but when my sister-in-law used the concrete patio for the butcher block and a dull cleaver, Don felt bad—as much for the chicken as for my sister-in-law. The next day when we went to a market, he made sure we bought them a new cleaver.

At the end of the trip, as we prepared to leave, everyone in my family was sitting around the living room crying. Don thought they were sad because we were going back to America and they'd miss us. I took a deep breath and explained the situation wasn't nearly as sweet as he imagined.

"No, they want us to help them out. My sister wants cows for her kids to raise to help them be more self-sufficient like I had helped Huy Van by buying him a van so that he could earn a living. She has also borrowed a lot of money and can't pay it back. Huy Van is also in debt, but not as much," I said. I was disappointed with them because they didn't seem to understand what seems so obvious to me: you must live within your means. I knew that they had very few opportunities, but I had been helping them out for years. Don just listened to me vent, letting me get it all out.

What especially upset me was that Huong, my sister, who is beautiful, looked like a homeless person. She was out of work because the growth in factories made her tailoring work unnecessary. Nobody wanted her custom-sewn clothing. I felt bad for her when I arrived, so I took her shopping and bought her a necklace, earrings, and a bracelet, which I specifically told her not to pawn. I bought her pretty clothing so she would look good going to weddings and funerals.

Because we know the importance of being self-sufficient, Don and I decided to help her children by giving them what they needed to buy the cows to raise. The choice was encouraging and showed us that they had the correct attitude. We also gave my sister enough money to pay off her debts with some extra to give her a base to build from, but I made it clear that it was to be used for these purposes, and she agreed to the condition.

As Huy Van drove us to the airport I reminded him to make sure that our gifts to my sister and children were used as intended. I reminded him how his life had improved because of this van we were driving in. Now he had a means to earn a living and had been able to get married and have a son. I was okay helping out as long as everyone was taking steps to improve their lives. Otherwise, if at the end of the day nothing changed for the better, what was the point. Huy Van said he understood and would remind my sister.

Don and I said our goodbyes and then went into the terminal. On the flight home I told Don, "Well you wanted to see my family and that's what you got."

"Yes, I just wasn't expecting to see them that much. I now know that when I'm listening to you I need to be on guard against my assumptions coloring what you say. Well . . . I wanted to see your family with you, and we did that. I still think it was important for you and for us to do. Overall, I think it was a good honeymoon. Unconventional, but good."

After Don and I arrived back in Texas, my mom asked for details about the trip and everyone back home. As I told her what the family was doing I let her know the help we gave them, and she seemed happy about it.

Later, my mom heard through the Vietnamese grapevine that my sister had immediately pawned the jewelry and she and her children used the cow money and the debt repayment money to buy themselves fancy motorcycles. When she told me, I lost it. I let my mom know how disappointed I was that my sister betrayed me and my intention to help her get back on her feet. That she broke my heart and humiliated me in front of my husband.

"If I can learn that you don't buy things when you don't have money, why can't they do that as well?" I said. "All these years I've been in America, we've been living on a shoestring, and sending much of what I have saved to them—and the money is worth way more there. We have done without things we wanted so I could send money home, because I knew they needed the help, but they waste it on useless things just to show off. Do they not respect my sacrifices? Our sacrifices? Do they not care? When they waste money like this, they waste the opportunity to stand on their own feet and make their lives better." This last part really hit home with my mom, and she called my sister to chew her out. Later my brother called me and let me know that my sister was mad at me for causing my mom to be upset with her.

"Tell my sister to never call me again," I said. "I'm done."

My sister and I have talked once since then, and she apologized. Later, my niece called me and said their roof was leaking. Don convinced me to give my niece one more chance to make a good decision, so we sent them the money for the repairs. From what we heard, they did use the money fix their roof.

Our honeymoon was nothing like the blissful experience most newlyweds expect. Ironically, this time did help Don and I form a stronger relationship, although that bond didn't grow under an arch of roses in front of a tropical sunset as we gazed longingly into each other's eyes. Put under pressure, two people figure out what kind of couple they are going to be. Spend twenty-four hours crammed in a hot van with screaming kids, and you know exactly what breaks your partner—or in Don's case, *doesn't* break your partner. I can't say I would do it again, but I can say that the optimist in me was glad to know early what kind of person would be sharing my path with me.

Twenty-One

Don calls my way of tackling life my "chop-chop" approach. It's funny, the way he says it, but it's true. I like to have as much fun as the next person, and I love to laugh. But I don't put up with foolishness, as anyone who knows me can tell you. When I know what needs to be done, you better get out of my way.

Coming home from our Vietnam trip, I was more convinced than ever about the kind of life—the kind of foolishness—I did not want for my family and me. I explained to Don how important it was to me that my family be one that functions with integrity. I knew he'd understand, since he feels exactly the same way.

"Even when I was little, it really turned me off to see my brother and sister showing off," I told Don one evening, soon after we were home from the exhausting honeymoon. "I would see my mom struggling to buy things that my siblings thought they needed, so they could impress people."

"How did your mom feel about that?" Don asked me.

"She hated it. She was so upset, feeling like she let them down. She worked so hard but they felt like it was never enough. I will never be like that, and I won't let my family be like that."

I felt this kind of showing off was linked to an even greater sin, coveting what isn't yours. I've had clients who have left diamond rings on my table by accident, and when they do, I usually call them and tell them I'll drop it off to them. They've never worried whether I would actually do it. Once a customer called me after she'd left her appointment.

"Sau, I've lost a beautiful ring," the lady said, going on to describe it.

"Oh, no! It isn't here. And you know that I'll always call you if you've left anything here."

"I know that, but I'm just trying to remember every place I've been, so I thought I'd just check," she said.

When she couldn't find the ring, she filed a claim with her insurance company. A whole year later, she found it—and even before she called the insurance company to set up a repayment, she called me to tell me the news. I was touched that she thought of me.

Sau doing nails at her new salon. *Photo by Dee Dee Flores.*

Even though many of my clients are the types of people who have expensive diamond rings, they don't show off with their money. They have always been so inclusive of me, bringing me into their vacations, their homes, their lives. They treat others with dignity and respect, and those are the kinds of people I want in my home and in my life. My theory is that if you put on airs, it will catch up with you. When you do the right thing, when you work toward the right goals in life, eventually your dreams will come to you. That's something that my own siblings haven't figured out yet.

Not one day goes by that I don't thank God that I got to come to this country and experience this life I treasure. Every day I get up and come to work with a smile on my face, and every day, I work to figure out how to better adapt to the American lifestyle. I want to incorporate as much of my new country into my home and family as possible. Moving to America is one thing, but adopting the *culture*, especially when it's so different from your own, is something entirely different—it takes time and effort, an open mind, and a willingness to practice, I assure you.

Shortly before Don and I got engaged, the gratitude I felt for my clients and my new life here was overflowing, and what was coming up on the calendar? Thanksgiving, that most American of all American holidays. I started thinking about how much I wanted to celebrate it the right way this year. I had been in America for years, for goodness sake, and I hadn't hosted a traditional Thanksgiving dinner for anyone yet. I was determined that this year would be different.

Our first Thanksgiving in the United States, we did absolutely nothing.

We'd been here about six months and hadn't had time to learn much about American holidays. When the hotel where I was working gave everyone a big turkey to take home and prepare, nobody really explained what to do.

"This chicken is way too big for our family!" my mom told me, shaking her head.

"Do whatever you can," I told her, not knowing what else to say.

So she cut off a turkey breast and boiled it, shredding it and seasoning with salt and pepper and herbs, just like we do chicken in the Vietnamese way. We couldn't figure out why this giant chicken was an important function the fourth Thursday in November.

Later when I was working in a salon, one of my customers, Terri, asked me if my mom, Scott, and I celebrated a traditional American Thanksgiving.

"I'm not sure what you mean by 'traditional American Thanksgiving,'" I said. Then I explained how we had been preparing the turkey. She seemed horrified.

"Boiled turkey! No, no, no!" She said, shaking her head. "I know what I can do for you. Let me take care of it for this year." She did that by ordering a prepared dinner that was delivered to our house on the Wednesday of Thanksgiving week.

My cell phone rang while I was at the salon on Wednesday afternoon. It was my mom.

"Sau, a lot of food has just arrived at our house. I don't know what it is or what we should do with it. Is this a mistake?"

"No. It is our first American Thanksgiving. I'll figure out what to do when I get home."

Once I got home, I stared at all the containers stacked on the counters in our tiny kitchen. There were more than a dozen boxes of food, in all sizes. We had no idea what to do with it all, nor did we understand why there was enough food for twenty or thirty people when there were just three of us. We called everyone we knew and shared the food, which I now understand is the spirit of Thanksgiving. I got it right without really knowing it at the time.

When my Hawaii trip with Don was coming up, I was ready to embrace all things American and have a huge Thanksgiving at my place. My goal was to make it a really special holiday, our first together. I was so excited to share this lovely American tradition with him. To me, this was exactly the kind of occasion worth celebrating, filled with the kind of sentiment that makes our life in this country so meaningful. So, humbled by what our life has given us here, I set out do Thanksgiving in a letter-perfect way.

Because my mom and I certainly weren't experienced American cooks, I decided it was best to order it from a reliable restaurant. I placed the order in plenty of time; all we had to do is pick up the dinner. The table was all set when Don arrived on Thanksgiving at noon, and we set out for the restaurant. We picked up big bags full of our fabulous dinner, and the bag I carried was hot and smelled good. How wonderful, I thought! It's like magic—the perfect Thanksgiving dinner, and I don't have to worry about cooking.

Back home, I unpacked my bag while Don unpacked the others. As he reached in the bag, he said that the dishes were ice cold.

"Stop kidding me. I don't need any stress at the moment."

"Sau, I'm not kidding."

"Yeah, right."

He picked up some printed instructions and start reading.

"First," he said, and then paused for a long time, "defrost the turkey." Pause. "When the turkey is defrosted, set the oven to 350 degrees." Pause. "Do you want me to read the rest?"

I was stunned into silence. Then I yelled, "Are you kidding me? Stop that right now! That's not funny. I ordered a fully cooked meal."

Don just turned his calm, sweet face to me and said, "It's a cooked turkey that's been frozen. The vegetables are hot, but nothing else. It's okay, it will just take longer and we will eat later. Let's preheat the oven."

"We don't have an oven."

"Yes, you do, it is right there."

"The oven doesn't work, only the top burners."

"You got to be sh!+!ng me."

"This is insane. This is Thanksgiving Day? Even *I* know you don't sell someone a frozen cooked turkey on Thanksgiving Day."

"Okay, Sau, let's call the restaurant and see if there's some mistake," Don suggested, trying to keep me calm while Scott tried to figure out when he would get his turkey and dressing, which he had been waiting patiently for all day.

I knew I risked Don seeing a side of me that wasn't pretty. My chop-chop attitude was in overdrive. But I was beyond caring about that; I thought my blood would boil. I called the restaurant and the person who answered said I could bring the turkey back and they'd cook it for me. Which meant our dinner would happen in the evening? Great.

We returned to the restaurant and asked for the manager. We told him we were the ones who had called earlier about cooking our frozen turkey.

"Sorry, but we just shut down all of our ovens and are getting ready to close and go home.

"But you said on the phone that you would cook this frozen turkey you sold us. What can we do?"

"We can refund your money."

"The money doesn't solve anything. You just ruined Thanksgiving for my family. You advertised a fully cooked meal and that is what I expect. When I ordered the meal, I had asked the person what I would need to do when I picked it up, and they told me all I need to do was pick up the meal and serve the food."

"I'm sorry. All I can do is refund your money."

Don put his hand on my arm. "Sau, there is nothing that these incompetent people can do, and it is getting late. Just take the refund for now and deal with this later so that we can find somewhere else to get food."

This Thanksgiving was going from bad to worse, and it was only 2:00 p.m.

All I could think about was that poor Scott would be horribly disappointed. During the last few years in America, he'd come to love the idea of a big Thanksgiving dinner.

Don was determined to make me happy and to feed Scott, so he took the matter in hand.

"Let's go find dinner. There has to be something open," he said.

After going to several places that were closed, Don took us to what seemed like a sure bet, Luby's, or at least our last hope. We arrived to find a huge line of people streaming out the front door, wrapping around the building. Apparently, Luby's is a primary destination for Thanksgiving dinner.

When we joined the line, I sized up the customer base: it was all single dads with kids. I began listening to them and realized that everyone had ordered dinners ahead of time; they were in line with their tickets in hand simply to pick up the prepared dinners to take home. My heart sank. I was the only woman in the line and felt so embarrassed that I wasn't prepared.

We stood in line until about 5:00 p.m., by which time smoke was shooting out of my ears. My hope, my dream, my best intentions for a perfect American holiday with the man of my dreams, all spoiled.

Don, ever the calm and reasonable sort, was afraid I was going to lose it. "Let me handle this," he said.

As we reached the front of the line, Don didn't even get a chance to speak before the guy behind the counter asked for our order receipt. He looked up and must have seen the expression on my face and the tears forming.

"Honey," he said, "don't even tell me about it. Let me go in the back and see what I have."

"Whatever you have, we'll take it."

He came back with a whole Thanksgiving dinner, saving the day. Well, sort of. When we returned home at 6:00 p.m., Scott had given up and had already eaten something my mom fixed for him. But Don and I finally sat down to a Thanksgiving dinner together.

"Sau," he said around a mouthful of turkey, "at some point we need to get you an oven."

Thanksgivings in the future, of course, would be far less dramatic. After we got married and built our first house, we had two ovens installed in the kitchen so we could easily make turkey and everything else for Thanksgiving. Don takes great pride in doing the turkey, which he brines in beer, lemon, orange, salt, and pepper. It's a hefty portion of American culture I savor with immense gratitude each and every year. And with my chop-chop approach in place, it comes off without any surprises.

Twenty-Two

Wanting our family to grow, Don and I built a home that would accommodate us, Scott, my mom, and another child. It was time to get pregnant.

I quit birth control pills and immediately had strange symptoms and very weird periods. Feeling hot flashes at age thirty-two wasn't right at all. Telling myself my body was probably just in shock from stopping the birth control pills, I sought out a new doctor. After an exam and some blood work, the office called me in for a visit to review the findings.

"I'll get right to the point," the doctor, a friendly but no-nonsense woman, said. "You're not going to get pregnant."

"What are you saying? I'm healthy. I've had a baby—I know I can get pregnant." I was so annoyed with the ridiculous conversation that my fists were clenched in my lap.

"I've run your tests three times. Your hormone levels indicate that you're in early menopause."

"This is crazy. It's wrong. It *has* to be wrong," I argued, my voice rising. "I'm thirty-two and menopause is twenty years away."

"I'll tell you what. You're understandably upset. Can you come back with your husband? I'd like to talk to both of you and see if I can make this make sense for you," she suggested.

Walking out of the doctor's office onto the burning pavement, I immediately began to sweat, although it wasn't entirely from the July heat, I pulled my phone out of my purse and called Don immediately. Furious and confused, I babbled at him the words the doctor said.

"This makes no sense," Don said. "You have periods!"

But he returned to the doctor's office with me a few days later, where the doctor told him the same thing. She said that a fertility specialist might have some good ideas, so she referred us to one she said is the best in town.

Visiting the specialist, we felt like there had to be some good news. But this doctor reviewed the test results—all three versions of the test results—and agreed with the first doctor.

"You're not going to get pregnant in any traditional way," he began. And with that, I watched as my husband turned green. Then his eyes rolled back in his head, and he slid to the floor from his chair.

I started screaming, "Don! Don! Oh God, what's happening?"

The doctor, cool as a cucumber, walked around his desk, patted me on the arm, and took Don's wrist in his hand to feel his pulse. As he did, he continued to talk to me about the test results and what he could do next.

"I don't care about the tests. Is my husband okay?" I was still shouting, but I didn't care.

"Please don't worry. This happens all the time. He's okay and you need to be calm."

Don's eyelids fluttered open and he focused on my face. "What happened?"

"You're giving me a heart attack," I told him, pulling him back into his chair. The doctor returned to his desk.

"You're possibly in premature menopause," the doctor said, "but I want to do a sonogram to look at your ovaries."

"What happens in early menopause?" I asked him. "How does that happen? What happens to your body?" I still couldn't wrap my mind around the idea of a thirty-two-year-old body acting like a fifty-year-old body.

"If you are in early menopause, then the sonogram should show that your ovaries have shrunk and look like small white balls."

"I only have one ovary," I explained, filling the doctor in on my emergency surgery almost a decade earlier. I told him about the cyst and the complications. "The doctor removed one of my ovaries and told me to start taking birth control pills to allow my remaining ovary to heal, which I did faithfully until we decided to have a baby." The doctor listened, a strange look on his face, and then he suggested that if I'd had cyst problems earlier, perhaps the sonogram would show that it was happening again.

The sonogram did, in fact, show what appeared to be a cyst and some small nubs that could be shriveled ovaries. An outpatient surgery was scheduled. When that procedure was finished, Don and I received the most awful news yet.

"You need to look at these pictures," the doctor said, placing black, gray, and white images in front of us on his desk. "Both your ovaries are gone."

"What? No, that's wrong," I said. "I was left with one ovary."

"And I'm showing you that you have no ovaries." He pointed to the image. "There is a clean cut where both of your ovaries should be. When a patient has cysts on both ovaries, which may have been your case, a doctor is obligated to give you the option to keep or not keep one ovary," he continued. "Were you not told you had a choice?"

"I was so sick and in so much pain that my surgery was done almost as soon as I went into the ER. I had blacked out. When I woke up, surgery had already happened."

The doctor looked at me with gentle eyes and nodded.

"I guess he lied to me about leaving me with an ovary," I said.

All those years ago, that original doctor had carried his lie further. He told me I needed to take birth control pills to keep my hormones working properly. Really, he wanted me to take the pills to keep me having regular periods. At this moment, I was stunned. I had always respected doctors, but now I felt completely betrayed and cold inside. I was lost.

This kindly fertility doctor looked at Don, who was still and quiet beside me—but still conscious, thank God—and then he looked at me.

"That is outrageous. That doctor should not be in practice. What was done to you is wrong. I'm a doctor and I never recommend legal action, but this is different. I will testify for you in court if you want me to."

We told him we couldn't wrap our heads around that at the moment, and asked what options, if any, we had to have a baby. The doctor explained the pros and cons of every procedure available to us. One option was in vitro fertilization, since my uterus was still healthy and I had already had one successful childbirth. Based on what we had explained to him earlier, he thought this might be the best option for us. He understood that we had just been through an emotional shock and told us to go home and take some time to think about what we wanted to do.

Driving back to our home, I was quiet, and Don was lost in his own thoughts as well. Inside the house, I put down my purse and sat on the couch. Don sat next to me. He took me by the hand, pulling me closer to sit beside him. He took one of my hands in his and wrapped his other arm around my waist.

"As long as we have each other, that's the most important thing," he said softly in my ear. "That's all the really matters to me."

We let the news settle and then began to research alternatives. The specialist had suggested the idea of in vitro to us. He believed in its success rate. But I was skeptical and scared. First, I was afraid of manipulating nature. And I worried that something would go wrong with that procedure for either me or the baby.

While we wondered if having a baby simply wasn't meant to be, I kept circling back to the guilt I felt. I felt awful that I'd married Don when I couldn't have more kids, but Don reassured me over and over that he understood. He knew I had no idea about this when we met.

"I know you want a baby," I told him. "I know how important having a family is to you, and that this horrible doctor's lie puts you and me in a horrible position. If he had told me the truth, I would have been able to forgive him because he was trying to save my life. I would have known what my options were, and I could prepare for my future. But his lie to save himself has put me in a difficult position. Unknowingly, I *lied* to you."

I could see from his expression that he didn't blame me, but I couldn't stop myself. Once I'd started spilling those poisonous emotions, I had to keep going.

"This whole thing has left me in shock and in sorrow," I said. "On one hand I don't want to mess with nature, and on the other hand, I don't want to not fulfill my obligation to you, the man I married. This weighs heavily on me. You didn't ask for this. I would understand if you wanted to leave me so that you can have a baby on your own, with someone who can have a baby." As I said this last sentence, I felt my heart squeeze painfully. This was it, the last of the poison, my greatest fear—that in the end, those school children were right, and someone this wonderful didn't want me after all.

Don took my hand. "Sau, I love you, and only you. I married you because I want to spend the rest of my life with you. Yes, I want a baby, but a baby only if I can have one with *you*. I didn't marry you just to have a baby. The most important thing is that we have and love each other. A baby would be a gift beyond what you have already given me."

This is the moment I turned my head around. I knew at that moment that Don really loved me. I need to be open minded about what our options were. I needed to think about his needs—not just mine. We needed to put the future of our family in God's hands.

* * * *

Eventually we decided to proceed with the in vitro option. Then a staggering thought occurred to me.

"With in vitro, we could have twins or triplets—or more," I said to Don one evening, during our many talks. "Can we handle that?"

"Sau, who knows what will happen? If we go with the minimum they suggest, two embryos, there's a chance that neither will take. If they are healthy, then there's a good chance at least one will take. Implanting two embryos gives us a 30 percent chance of having twins. The downside is that there is also a chance that the embryos could split and then we could have four children. Four! Can you imagine?"

No, I couldn't imagine, and I didn't want to.

"I think we need to put it in God's hands and only go with one embryo. If we don't get pregnant with one, perhaps it wasn't meant to be. I can live with that. Can you?"

"Yes, I can live with this decision," I said, but I was still getting used to how much Don was invested in *our* happiness, not just his. Putting the procedure in God's hands made me feel comfortable that we weren't doing anything unnatural. Once again, I was amazed at his selflessness. I realized I needed to turn my head around and let go of my fears, so I prayed hard that God would show us if a pregnancy was meant to be. It was clear to me

149

now that Don's prayers were the same.

Calling the specialist, we set up the in vitro process. Then the day came when it was time to implant our fertilized egg.

Don and I arrived at the specialist's office, and they placed us in separate waiting rooms. The nurse walked us through how the procedure was going to take place and said that we would have about an hour to talk through any final decisions about how many embryos we wanted to implant. We said that we already decided to implant only one.

She stopped midstep and turned around. "One! That's not recommended. Did they fully explain to you the chances of success? You don't get your money back if you don't get pregnant," she said, eyes serious and unblinking. "Two or three is best. Your odds for success are far greater. We have never implanted only a single embryo before. Please take your time to think carefully about this."

"That's fine for other people," Don told her. "We want just one egg."

Relenting, the doctor implanted one egg. On the way home, I kept asking Don if he saw the doctor actually put anything in me because I didn't really feel anything. He said, yes, as best he could tell.

And we did get pregnant.

It was an easy pregnancy, except for the first few months during which I needed to take shots until my body fully took over. Our beautiful baby girl, Sydney, came in mid-July, right on time. The miracle of my life, the hope that had only flickered at moments in my life, was alive in a blaze of joy.

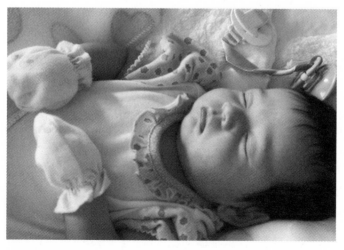

Baby Sydney home from the hospital. *Photo by Don Hudecek.*

Grandma trying to get Sydney to sleep.
Photo by Don Hudecek.

Baby Sydney taking a nap in Grandpa's arms. *Photo by Don Hudecek.*

Sau and Sydney enjoying Sydney's first trip to the beach. *Photo by Don Hudecek.*

Twenty-Three

My son was eighteen months old when we arrived in America. His name was Phuoc Nguyen, and until my neighbor, who loved my little boy dearly, told me to change his name, such an idea never occurred to me. This neighbor and friend shocked me with such a suggestion, but she was wise in the ways of America.

"Children will have a hard time pronouncing Phuoc Nguyen," she told me, "and will maybe say it like another word. One that you don't want."

Another friend said that Scott was a good name for a boy. I thought about it with my typical chop-chop attitude and said okay, that's good. It's easy to pronounce. So when he was four and headed off for his first day of pre-K, Phuoc became Scott Phuoc Nguyen.

He was starting school when his father and I were splitting up. Scott lived with my mom and me, so of course his childhood was totally different from what Sydney's would be. He had to learn to read and write English at school with no real help from me. I remember the day he came home from school so excited because he could now read and write English. I was so happy—it was a miracle. He could help me with my speaking skills. Today, he and Don and Sydney help me out all the time.

Though I always worked like mad to provide a good life for Scott, my mom, and me, Scott's childhood bore its difficulties. For example, the grandmother of one of Scott's friends would pick him up to take him to soccer because I was working every day of the week, and my mother could not drive. Scott had to fend for himself a lot. Looking back, I wish I could have spent more time with him during his early years, but I believe I made the best decision available to me at the time for his long-term well-being. I am certain that the way I raised him made him more independent, more resourceful. It's how I grew up with my mother, a single mom. We learned life skills early, and we were stronger for it.

My way of raising my son didn't seem abnormal to me until I listened to my customers' stories. I would hear them talk about being with their kids 24-7, which was a foreign concept to me. I'd never known such a life.

Naturally, I wished I could spend more down time with him and attend more of his games, but that option wasn't really available to me.

When he was in middle school and playing football in the afternoons, it still wasn't possible for me to simply leave work to see him play. It came down to this: do I work to pay the electric bill, or do I go watch a game? He'd be sad when I missed match after match, and I'd have to do my best to explain again why I felt my decision was the right one.

"I work hard to make money so we have what we need. Your job is to do well in school, behave, do what your teachers say to do," I told him, more than a few times. "You are to follow all the rules because I don't have time to come to the school to talk about any conflicts you might have."

He was always good. Every day I reminded him that school was his job. "Do not make me hear from your teacher," I would tell him. "Listen and do well in class." I said it so much that every day as I pulled up to the school to drop him off, he would look at me, taking the words out of my mouth: "Scott, school is your job." He would say it so I didn't have to.

When I was single and dating, I almost never let my dates meet me at home because I didn't want Scott to worry or wonder. But there was the rare exception to my rule. A long time before I met Don, I agreed to a blind date with an older doctor, a very old-fashioned gentleman who insisted on picking me up at my home. When Scott laid eyes on him, he was very uncomfortable, pacing back and forth until he pulled me into another room.

"Mom, have you lost your mind?" he nearly yelled at me. "He is way too old for you!"

I went to dinner anyway, but all I could do was stare at his gray hair. He was older than my mom, more than twice my age. I couldn't hear a thing the man said throughout dinner because Scott's words were ringing in my head. My son was right, of course. I would have been out of my mind to date this guy again.

But after several dates with Don, when I let him pick me up at home, Scott's face lit up. He liked Don instantly. "Much better," Scott whispered to me. When I told Scott that Don had never been married and didn't have kids, Scott actually gave a thumbs-up.

Now, I know what a pleasure it is to raise Sydney with a partner who supports you mentally and financially. I look back and wish Scott had had that kind of life; maybe if he had, he would have enjoyed life a little bit more. When he was little, Scott would ask me, "Where's my dad, why doesn't he show up for my soccer or my football games?" and I wouldn't know what to say.

When Scott was just in second grade and beginning to play soccer, with neither Dad nor Mom at his games, it was a sad situation. I can't do anything to fix that now, but it's still hard to look back at Scott's life, knowing what my own hurt was like without a dad, knowing how painful it was to

Scott holding Sydney for her first steps in ocean water.
Photo by Don Hudecek.

look around and see friends having a good relationship with two parents. I wanted that then for myself, and I wanted that for Scott. Just as my mom loved me and worked hard to give the best she could, I tried to do the same for my son.

For a time, I stayed with Scott's father, sacrificing my own happiness in order to give my son two parents. But then I realized you have to have two people working together to provide a child with a happy environment, and Scott's father and I didn't have a healthy relationship like that. Once I met and fell in love with Don, I finally understood a healthy relationship isn't about threats. It's about understanding each other.

And although I worried a lot about Scott not having a relationship with his biological father, Don has been very, very good with Scott. How I wish Don and I had met sooner. But from the moment he came into our lives, Don's participation has been full-on. His love for and support of Scott has been complete. And that goes back to Don's family, the genuine kindness and generous spirit they have and how much they value family. As soon as they met, Don's father treated Scott like his own grandson. When we have flown him up to Michigan for vacations, they've always made him feel included and completely at home. And I know this will make Scott a better parent when he has children.

In the end, I can't say that Scott got everything he wanted, but he did get everything he needed, including my love and support, and my belief in him. I hope he understands that even when I couldn't be with him, my heart was there, sitting in the stands, cheering him on and pushing him to be the best he could be.

* * * *

As Scott grew up, I began to worry about him and girls. Because I didn't grow up in a country where you turned on the TV and could watch sex and drug use on so many shows, it terrified me that Scott saw all this, all the time. I was so scared, forever telling him not to do anything that would make him lose control. I know he got tired of hearing me, but I believe that if you stay on top of things, talk about the difficult issues with your child, you'll come out ahead.

"It's good to remember that everything you do has a consequence," I told him, maybe a thousand times. "You always have to be cautious and careful. You don't want to get in money troubles, and that's why it's important that you balance our family checkbook."

I explained the difficulties in raising a child and how a teen pregnancy would be a disaster. I told him that falling in love with a wonderful woman is a good goal, for later. I couldn't emphasize enough how getting in trouble would mess up his entire life.

He nodded. He obeyed. But I could tell he was really tired of hearing it. He even told me I was being too hard on him. But if I was sure of anything, it was that being his best friend was not my job. Teaching him to do everything for himself was far more important, so he learned to do his laundry, clean the whole house, and cook like a pro in the kitchen. I can remember a thirteen-year-old Scott telling me I was terrible for forcing him to be so grown up. And then there was the college-aged Scott, who thanked me for teaching him how to take care of everything.

Over the years, my conversations with people who are sweet, kind, and intelligent people have made me very aware that we have different perspectives on some parts of life. I've heard horror stories of people who should have everything going for them winding up in trouble with drugs, depression, and financial ruin. And I found myself terrified of what could be out there, what Scott might run into down the road.

About the time Scott was fourteen, he sat me down for a serious talk, instead of the other way around. "You and my grandmother did a great job of raising me, but you have to give me a little bit of freedom, a little bit of room to breathe," Scott said, all wisdom and seriousness.

"What are you talking about? Are you nuts?" I asked him. "You're not old enough to make your own decisions. Are you crazy?"

"I'm just saying that I'm not a baby anymore. I will not go out and snort cocaine or put a gun to my head. You just have to trust me, and let me make my own mistakes so that I can learn from them," he said.

All I could do was freak out, fearing that he must be about ready to throw his life away with some catastrophe. I was so frightened of what could go wrong for Scott, no matter how focused I was on instructing him on his choices.

Talking over my fears with Don, we decided to attend a parenting class at our church. The first meeting we went to, we heard awful stories of sad situations. We listened to the moderator's advice. We were quiet, taking it all in. On the drive home, I turned to Don from my place in the passenger's seat.

"We are taking seats away from people who need this class," I said. Don nodded in agreement.

But Scott could tell I was still worried. He volunteered to go to counseling with me if it would make me feel better. How mature he is, I thought.

I found a specialist who works with teens and their families. I explained to the therapist that Scott's father never participated in his life after we split up and that I was very concerned he didn't know how much he is loved.

The counselor listened with a thoughtful expression. "Let me have a little time with Scott alone. Is that okay?"

"Yes, please, take as long as you need."

I went into another room while he talked with Scott, wishing I could hear what they were saying. A half an hour later, Scott came out and said, "The counselor wants to talk to you."

I sat down in the chair opposite the counselor's desk. I waited for him to speak, too nervous to speak.

The counselor said, "Mom, you have a problem."

"Yes, I know. What can we do to fix it?"

"You have to give him a little room. I can assure you, you will not have a problem with this boy. He is a good son. If you try to protect him from everything, then he will have a problem," he said, smiling.

I let that sink in, relieved. Then I worried about my own sanity.

"Should I keep seeing you?" I asked.

"No, not unless you want to."

Scott and I walked to the car in silence. I thought to myself, okay, he's not a baby anymore. I have to turn this around.

"You know what?" I asked Scott, buckling my seat belt and starting the car. "You asked for responsibility and freedom. It will kill me if you do something you're sorry about, but you need some freedom and I'm going to let you make decisions for yourself."

He smiled and said, "Thank you."

But soon I could see from watching his body language—you know how macho boys want to be—that the burden was on his shoulders. I could see him thinking that he should have been careful what he asked for.

Observing him for the next couple of years until he graduated from high school was interesting. He had a curfew earlier than his friends, but he didn't seem to mind. Don and I gave him a cell phone, and when he went over his minutes, first we asked him to pay attention to his usage, but eventually I had to take the phone away to get the message across. After a couple of weeks of coming home and seeing the phone still in the drawer, I thought, wow, he's doing great!

I felt so proud and let Don know how well Scott was following our rules. Then the bill came in and Don said this was not the case.

"What do you mean? His phone is still in the drawer."

Don got Scott's phone and opened it up. He showed me that the SIM card was gone.

"But his phone is right there. How can he place calls without his phone?"

Don called Scott down and said, "Scott, before you answer the question I'm about to ask you, consider that your punishment will be ten times worse if I catch you lying to us. Now . . . do you have another phone that you put your SIM card in?"

Scott looked at Don, scared and confused. "Yes. But how did you know?"

"I have tried everything that you will ever think of trying, so I know how to think like a teenager who thinks he is smarter than his parents."

Scott went upstairs and brought down the other phone. We confiscated that one in the drawer as well.

"You can't do that," he said. "It belongs to my friend."

"Well, that is your responsibility to take care of," Don said, "and now you're grounded from using your phone for an extra two weeks."

I was furious and wanted to punish him even more. I sat him down and yelled at him, but Don calmed me down, wanting me to put things in perspective.

"Sau," Don said, "this is very minor. It's not the end of the world. Let's wait for something important before we get upset and talk about sending him off to military school."

Don, naturally, was right. Scott has always been good at following rules. He's made good decisions. At least for someone his age. He takes responsibility seriously and graduated from high school early by accelerating his classes. After that, he earned his bachelor's degree from the University of Arkansas, where he met the beautiful young woman who has now become his wife.

Just as I was breathing a sigh of relief that my son had turned into a good man, he began considering an idea that made me afraid I would lose him forever. There was a time, briefly, after college graduation, when Scott thought very seriously about joining the Marine Corps. I was truly

Scott and Win taking their first steps in life as husband and wife.
Photo by Eileen Thurman.

terrified of my son being shipped out to a war zone. But Scott, a truly thoughtful and grateful young man, presented a good argument to me.

"This wonderful country we came to has given us so much. I want to give back. I believe it's the right thing to do," Scott told me when I confessed my fears. "If we'd stayed in Vietnam, we would have missed out on an incredible life. I'm an American and I want to do my part."

As I listened to him, I was flooded with pride. This was the man I had raised. "You're right. Joining the military isn't wrong. I'm proud of you for

Sau and Scott at the center of the United States Capitol Crypt.
Photo by Don Hudecek.

feeling that way and I know that serving the country would make you feel like you're a better citizen. But getting a job and paying taxes that support the military and social services—that's also doing your part." Even though I was impressed by his sense of civic duty, you can't blame a mother for trying a little logic to keep a son out of the line of fire.

As I started to contemplate the idea of my son following in my father's footsteps and becoming a soldier, I began to think a great deal about America and its connection to my old country. So many in the United

States believe that its military was a monster in Vietnam, a vicious force whose true motivations lay in the shadows. Most of those people didn't live for almost two decades in the DMZ like I did, although some may have fought on the front lines of that terrible war. Most of those people didn't understand what life was like for us, and it's easy to be self-righteous from a comfortable seat in front of a television.

Ultimately, although the Americans were not able to liberate my country, I see them as heroes. They came to Vietnam to help people like my mother who had to search the rice fields at night to feed her children. They came to Vietnam to destroy a government that keeps families like mine from ever tasting even the hope of success. They came to bring us freedom, and they bled all over our land in hopes that we, too, would one day have the freedom they enjoyed at home. Although I didn't want my son to join them in their graveyards, I couldn't have more gratitude for the sacrifice they made for us, no matter how hollow it must feel for their families.

In the end, Scott didn't join the marines. He decided to work instead for an architecture consulting firm in Arkansas; now he works at a software and web development company. He's a good young man and I couldn't be more proud. I would be just as proud if he had served in the military, of course. Maybe my relief about his chosen path comes from my lifelong fear of the terrors of war. Maybe I'll never disconnect from the trauma of losing my sister to a land mine. And maybe my parenting will always be about protecting my children from the heartbreaks and fears a young, scared girl experienced so many years ago.

Twenty-Four

Understanding my mother—who can seem very stubborn or difficult at times—comes more easily when you consider her early years. My mom endured a traumatic childhood. She lost her mother when she was eight, and her father beat her. Though she was abused, she never wanted to talk to me about it, so I found out about all her tragedies from neighbors and relatives. She was married at eighteen and had four kids. Her husband died when she was twenty-nine. There was always war, too—first with the French and then with the Americans. Nothing about her life was easy, peaceful, or happy.

It would be years into my adulthood before I could truly comprehend how her life affected my own worldview. Only with my own maturity could I come to see that I became so fixed in my ways because of the things she suffered. On one hand, her focus on providing for her family helped me develop my commitment to finding a new and better life. But I also knew that I would overcome obstacles rather than accept them, rather than let them hold me back the way they did my mother.

Because her experience pushed me to become the person I am, I was ready to fully embrace the innumerable opportunities found in my new American life. Yet incredibly, my mother felt little of the joy or fulfillment I had found. She had made friends at church, but she seemed to find no real pleasure in being in a new and exciting country. I was frustrated but unable to fix it, or so I thought.

It would take a crisis in my soul for me to finally understand an important truth: though our lives are forever intertwined, and though her long-ago choices eventually led me to this wonderful country, we are very separate people. I would have to find out the hard way that our relationship would require an infusion of real space for it to survive. In fact, the relationship had to implode for me to understand that what she needed was nothing like the life I was giving her.

When I was young, I hated to make her unhappy, so I tried not to grill her about my absent father or my circumstances. She lost a daughter, my beautiful, wonderful sister, and she also lost a son. My surviving brother and sister were so difficult with her, always wanting and demanding more, which she worked very hard to give to them. I resented their greed and lack of gratitude; as a result, when I was so unhappy about the way people treated me, I just suffered in silence. I didn't want to add to her sad load. That may have limited my ambition for a while, but not for long.

I had a step-grandmother who was very good to me and helped raise me because my mother was always working. I consider her my actual grandmother. She told me that before and after my father was in my mother's life, there were other men who wanted to date and marry her, but she wasn't interested. She was a worker who provided for her family. She's been single for much, much longer than she was ever married.

Although it wasn't happy, my mother's life in Vietnam was all she'd ever known. So after we'd been here in America for a few years, she really missed home and the friends and family she'd left behind. So in about 1997, we spent months and months planning her first trip home. Every time she would see a jacket or shirt she wanted to take back to people at home, she would buy it and squirrel it away in a suitcase. I too gave her things to take to the friends I loved and missed so much. Over the years, I would send her home to Vietnam several times, although I was not prepared for some of those experiences. To be honest, my mother sometimes tested my patience—to the ends of the earth.

One of my mother's trips home to Vietnam was not long after 9/11, when security changes became drastic. She wouldn't believe me when I told her she couldn't take everything she wanted. No large metal items, I told her, nor any of the safety pins she liked to use to hide money in her jacket and clothes. A tragedy like 9/11 made no sense to her, even when I explained it. It was as if it were a story unrelated to her, something from another world. Even as I became totally acclimated to American life, she remained completely removed from these realities.

As she packed, I gave her a money pouch Don had purchased for her to wear around her waist, and she had her shoulder bag also as her carry-on. Don wasn't sure she had understood my warnings, and right before we left for the airport, he asked me to check all of her luggage and her purse. I did. I even dumped everything out of her purse and put everything back in one item at a time. I told Don he shouldn't be so suspicious.

When we checked her luggage, I explained to the ticket agent that I'd need to walk my mother to her gate because she wouldn't be able to find it on her own. The airlines are usually good about this sort of thing, and she allowed me to go through security with my mom while Don and Scott remained outside. Going through security, however, it became abundantly clear all was not well. The TSA agents kept sending her carry-ons through the scanner again and again.

I looked at my watch. Gah! Time was ticking away, and my mother needed to board.

The scanning agent pulled us aside. "We see something significant on the x-rays but can't find anything upon inspection. We need to call the police and the head of DFW security."

We did not have time for this. "There's nothing but her wallet in her purse. I checked everything before we left for the airport."

The agent was unmoved by my explanation, which I guess is a good trait for TSA personnel. "Based on the x-rays, we know what is in the purse. We have inspected the purse but cannot get to the item because it appears to be in between the lining. We've looked for any hole or re-stitching, but could not find anything. We can't get to whatever it is. That is why I had to call the police and the head of security."

My watch was burning a hole in my wrist by this time, and my phone kept ringing. It was Don, trying to call me to see what was happening. He could see Mom and me, just on the other side of security, surrounded by about twenty people. Through the gaps in the plexiglass, Don yelled at me, "Answer the phone!" I could see it on his face. He was wondering if he needed to call a lawyer.

My mother looked at me innocently. "What's holding us up?"

I couldn't handle it anymore. These twenty people surrounding us, scratching their heads, needed to make something happen—*now*. "Look, my mom doesn't speak English very well, and she doesn't really know what is going on. She doesn't understand about 9/11 and all of the new security rules, but I assure you that she couldn't hurt an ant. I tried to explain to her that she couldn't bring anything. I thought she followed my instructions. I will take full responsibility for this. Just keep her purse, but please, please let her get on her plane. This trip means the world to her, and if she misses her flight you'll have a heart attack to deal with next. If you can't find any way to get at what you need, you have my permission to cut the lining of the purse to see whatever you think you see on the x-ray. "

"Are you sure?"

"I'm positive."

One of the policemen pulled out a knife and cut the lining. Out fell two knives. I could have died. I turned to look at my mother, my anger burning so hot I thought I might go off, right there in front of TSA security. But right now I needed to get her on the plane.

They looked at the knives and one of them asked me, "Who is Donald Anthony Hudecek?"

I was confused. "He's my husband, the one over there acting like a fool." I pointed to the other side of the plexiglass where Don was pacing and glaring at us. "Why?"

The policeman didn't answer me and took the knives to Don. They talked. When the policeman handed Don the knives, Don blew up. I can honestly say I've never seen my gentle Don that angry in my life. Later I learned that my mother had seen the knives in our closet and didn't think anyone was using them. What a fabulous gift, she thought. Always the smuggler, she sewed them carefully into the lining of her purse to keep the thieves away.

The policeman nodded to everyone on our side of security and let her get on her flight. They walked my mom and me to her gate, and she got on the plane. Luckily the flight was delayed, otherwise she would have missed it. Talk about a God thing.

The moment she walked out of my sight, I burst into tears. The weight of my frustrations with trying to make her understand the world we live in today simply overwhelmed me. I'd made it my mission to become an American in every way I possibly could, and in doing so, I felt the fear and sadness and outrage all Americans experienced with the horror and fallout of 9/11. That my mother could live in America with me, with our family, and enjoy the miraculously good life we do, yet not understand one of the most astounding changes in our world was beyond me.

Don traveled a lot for work and blamed my mom when he was selected for "random" inspections for the next three months. I was told the reason my mom was allowed to continue on her flight was that they were able to positively attribute the knives to someone. Don's name was engraved on one of the knives, which had been a Christmas gift to him when he was a teenager. This chance detail was lucky for my mom, but not so much for Don.

When she returned home, I told her how frustrated I was. "If you ever want to go to Vietnam again, you need to listen to me."

It was two years before I let Mom return to Vietnam. I was six months pregnant with Sydney and she wanted to visit Vietnam before I had the baby. My mom was returning home a week before my due date, and her return flight landed in Los Angeles, as before. That's where she changed planes, like before. But in LA, she refused to get on the plane to DFW.

The day she was to arrive home at DFW in the evening, I got a call at work in the afternoon. It was a flight attendant saying that my mom was refusing to get on her flight. I asked the flight attendant to give the phone to her.

"I'm back. Come get me. I'm here. We are in America," she said.

"You can't be home. Your plane isn't due for another five hours. You are in a different city."

She tried to convince me otherwise, and it took a few moments before I got the picture. She'd met some people on the plane from Vietnam and they lived in LA. They were home, so she thought she was home, too.

She simply said, "I'm tired and you need to come get me."

"You are not home. You are in Los Angeles, which is a three-hour flight from our home. Get on the plane that brings you here," I demanded.

"No, I'm home. Come pick me up."

"Mom, if I get in the car, it will be three days before I can get there. I am about to have a baby, which you know. I cannot drive to get you. Get on the plane!" I sighed with frustration and told her to give the phone back to the flight attendant.

"Listen to me!" I had to keep from screaming when I spoke to the airline representative at LAX. "I'm nine months pregnant. You have my permission to pick her up and throw her on the plane. Do whatever it takes, because I am not coming to get her." Of course, I was very emotional with hormones. Pregnancy can do that.

I guess they dragged her onto the plane, because she flew home to DFW.

I've asked Scott repeatedly if he would like to go to Vietnam. I really want him to understand where he's from, and he gets that. He's very curious, too, and he speaks fluent Vietnamese. But when I've suggested that he go on one of her return trips to Vietnam, he shuts down. All I get is, "NO!"

Like Don and me, Scott is beyond frustrated with my mother's refusal to open her mind to our American life. And he's not at all interested in experiencing the kind of drama we had at DFW that time, all those years ago. Her stubborn ways irritate him as much as they do Don and me.

Even family trips have become more trouble than they're worth, if Mom is involved. She becomes very difficult when it's time to go out to eat, insisting that she will only eat pork. In Chicago on vacation, this became a big issue. We sat in our hotel room, calling restaurant after restaurant to find those that served pork. When we'd eat in those restaurants, she would say, "The pork is no good here." It's a control thing, I think. She wants pork as it's cooked in Vietnamese culture, and that's that.

Don puts up with all this out of the goodness of his heart. There have been times I couldn't figure out how he manages to find such patience. Before we moved to our new home in Granbury, we were still living in Fort Worth in the house we built, and Mom was increasingly unhappy and difficult. She would meet me at the garage door when I arrived home from work to tell me about how everything in her world went wrong. Every single day. I would turn on music or go shut myself in the bedroom so I couldn't hear her.

I begged her, "Don't be ungrateful and miserable. Why can't you be happy? You have Vietnamese television and a phone to call home."

She complained about everything in our house, in our kitchen, in our lives, and I began to grow deeply resentful. She started to talk about moving out, but that made no sense to me. All I knew was that we were supposed to live together as long as she was alive. I thought she was losing her mind. It was absolutely a crazy idea.

When she couldn't convince me, she began to attack Don in her daily complaints to me. I thought I would lose it one afternoon when she began to accuse him of cheating. It was just the spice she needed for her ongoing tirade about her horrible life.

"You know your husband has three girlfriends?" She threw down a challenge she knew I wouldn't ignore.

I had been about to walk away from her toward our bedroom when the words sank in. I whirled around and stormed up to her, staring down at her.

"Are you insane?"

"He is a terrible husband. A cheat. He doesn't go to work. But he *is* on the phone, all day long. I listen on the phone. He is talking to all different women. Three women. You are a fool for trusting him," she said.

I just stared at her. Could she really be so clueless?

"He works at home! People work at home!" I said.

"No. No," she said. "You are stupid. Men go to an office to work. Your husband stays in this house on the telephone. I listen to his calls and tell him he is a cheat."

"He works on the telephone!" I said, trying not to scream. "He does business with people all over the country, and their meetings are on the phone. His clients are men and women. He has conference calls that last for hours at a time."

"You are wrong and you are blind," she said.

"If he didn't work as hard as he does, I promise you that we could not live in this nice house. I do fine at work, but Don makes good money with his business. He works long, hard days to earn the money for us to have all the wonderful things we do."

But nothing seemed to sway her. Everything in America, including my husband, was terrible, terrible, terrible.

Don, who was kind enough to take her to her doctor appointments while I was at the salon, even bought her vitamins. But she decided he was trying to poison her with pills. To say that her accusations upset him is an understatement. He'd built a nice house with her own mother-in-law suite, and she wasn't giving him any respect. She was truly ungrateful, Don was insulted and hurt, and I was caught in the middle.

The bottom fell out of my relationship with my mom the day I came home from work and found that she'd run away. She had a friend pick her up and told her friend not to tell a soul where she was. I was frantic by the third day. I finally called a friend of hers.

"If you know where she is, you need to tell me," I said. "I'm a wreck and I'm going to call the police."

Her friend caved in. "No, don't call the police. I know where she is. I also know that she really wants to move out of your house."

I was crushed. All I knew to do was go to church and get on my knees.

"Please, please, God, show me what to do," I wept. "I thought avoiding confrontation was the right thing. But today, I officially hand her over to you. You take care of my mother and tell me how to handle this."

When I returned home from church, I got a phone call from someone I didn't know. She was a friend of a friend in the Vietnamese community

The family enjoying a day in the park. *Author's collection.*

here in Fort Worth. She'd heard about my falling out with my mother.

"You and I are in the same situation," this woman explained to me. "After much frustration and many tears, I moved both of my parents into an apartment in Arlington where a lot of Vietnamese people live. All of them are hardheaded and stubborn and refuse to learn. And they like being together. They're all happy there."

I thanked her and hung up. Arlington is only about twenty minutes or so from where we lived in Fort Worth. It sounded crazy to me, a mother from my culture living on her own, but I didn't know what else to do. So I called the management for the apartments the woman told me about. They said I should come check it out, but they warned that they didn't offer assisted living. "Independent living only," they said, to which I replied, "Okay."

I called my mother's friend and told her my plan, and she put me in touch with my mom. I picked up my mother the next day and explained what I'd found out about the apartments in the Vietnamese community in Arlington. For the first time in perhaps years, I saw something like hope in my mother's face.

We drove to Arlington and found the apartments. As I pulled into the driveway, we could see a lot of Vietnamese people. Many of them were like her, older women dressed in the Vietnamese style. I turned to my mom to ask what she thought, and I saw it, the beginning of a miracle: she had a big smile on her face.

"This is good. I will live here," she said.

"Well, wait," I said. "We don't know if there's anything available. The management has to see if they think you qualify."

As soon as the managers met her, they told us something was immediately available. She moved in right away, and this act changed everything. She immediately discovered that five widows lived within a stone's throw. They all go to church and the supermarket together. They walk around the complex together, sit on the porch, and talk. That's how our culture lives. That's how we grew up. I hadn't realized how isolated she was. And I deeply regretted not realizing it sooner.

I found myself back at church, on my knees. "God," I said, "I'm so sorry I waited so long to turn her over to you. I was being stubborn in wondering why she couldn't be happy. I was trying to give her things instead of realizing she needed human interaction with people she understands. I wasn't listening to what she needed."

It is all about the learning curve for me. Finally, I figured out how much better it is to just communicate, even if it means hearing something I might not want to hear. It's so much better for her, as well as for Don, Sydney, and me. We have our own lives, and that doesn't mean we don't love each other.

I wake up now thinking how good it feels. And when I see my mom, there's such a difference. She is so comfortable with people from her own culture. Today, she has that. She has real peace and happiness, finally. And she's even asked when Don might get her some more of those vitamins.

Twenty-Five

When I look back at the milestones in the journey that delivered me to my life today, I see that each step connects me more than the one before it to the identity I have found for myself here. I grow to understand each day that this journey had become a balancing act—holding in one hand my ever-shifting adjustment to a culture so radically different than the culture of my youth, while holding in the other my family, as all of us negotiate the ups and downs of our relationships with one another. I don't know whether to laugh or cry at all the learning and growing I had to do. All I know is that my gratitude is boundless.

Maybe the most important step in my transformation to the new me was becoming an American citizen. I was qualified to become a citizen, so I decided to study for the required test and submitted my paperwork. After the application was processed, I had to undergo interviews and verbal testing. There were about a hundred questions on my study list, and I didn't know which questions I would be asked. I was glad to do this. It's an important step, and everyone who comes here should learn about this new and wonderful country we call home.

I did well on the test, and the time came to be sworn in. It was a Saturday morning, and I was incredibly nervous and excited. Don was happy as he drove us to the ceremony in Dallas. Scott, as my minor child, would automatically become a citizen with me.

I was terrified we would be late, but that was just my nerves getting the best of me.

"Can you go any faster?" I asked Don, as we moved along with the relatively heavy traffic on Interstate 30, making our way from Fort Worth to Dallas. "What if we are late and I don't get to be a citizen?"

Don kept his eyes on the road, ever the safe driver. He reached his right hand across the console toward me, in the passenger's seat, and patted my arm to calm me. "We won't be late. You don't want me to speed and get stopped by a cop, right? Then we *would* be late."

I nodded and took a deep breath, trying to settle down. I turned to the back seat, where Scott was staring out the window to the right, looking at Six Flags Over Texas. I'm sure he would rather have gone there to ride the roller coasters instead of going to some building in Dallas, but I also knew that one day he would appreciate this moment, this rite of passage.

Then I looked at my mom, huddled in the other corner of the back seat. She was looking out the left window, probably at nothing. Her long face saddened me. I hated for anything to dampen the thrill I felt at becoming a real American, but I couldn't help but feel the disappointment that consumed her.

Mom so deeply wanted to become a citizen, too. She'd left behind her country and braved a new country to be with Scott and me, but she couldn't read or write English and couldn't pass the test. The situation had stressed us out—quite a bit. I knew she wouldn't pass, but I couldn't tell her not to try. When she received her results in the mail, she was heartbroken. It was much later that she would become a citizen: when immigrants in her situation have been here for fifteen years, they can take the test in their native language. But not being able to become a citizen alongside Scott and me was devastating to her.

The day went by in a blur: there were more than a hundred of us sworn in at the same time. I heard there were people from more than thirty different countries, all taking the oath of allegiance. I was awash in a sea of people smiling, hugging, crying, and taking photographs.

My heart feels overwhelmed even now at this amazing event. Our country has a big heart—I understood that from the get-go. For me, getting up each day, going to work, and paying taxes is how I can show the American people my gratitude, that I'm doing my part to earn this life. Paying America back for her generosity is the least I can do. As an immigrant, I think it's important to learn the language and embrace the culture of this new home and to show gratitude for the people who fought for freedom. And I want to help those who are going through the process I did when I arrived. I try to do that in the way I operate my business as a landlord. The houses I rent could fetch a higher rate than I charge, but I rent to low-income families at a very cheap rate. I think it's my responsibility to give a chance to those whose paychecks are small, so I make their rent very affordable. My hope is that they also feel gratitude for being able to live in this country.

I thank God for this mind-set. You have to be a self-starter to make something of yourself, and I am fortunate that I grew into this way of being. I can't understand people who are consumed with negativity. Sure, it's easy to let yourself get down by thinking you have nothing, but if poor people here could see how bad it is to be poor where I came from, maybe they could get a clue that they shouldn't be complaining. In fact, this country is so generous that sometimes I think we're giving too much to people who sometimes aren't earning it. The Declaration of Independence says we have the right to pursue happiness, which requires action on our part

Sau's family in front of the United States Capitol building. *Author's collection.*

At the World War II memorial. *Author's collection.*

Sau, Scott, and Sydney next to the Lincoln Memorial Reflecting Pool.
Photo by Don Hudecek.

Sau and Sydney honoring Lincoln.
Photo by Don Hudecek.

to acquire. Happiness is not something that is the government's responsibility to ration out like a bread line. Opportunity doesn't come easily; you have to work for it.

Here, you can be poor and have electricity, but where I come from, poor people have a candle, and that's it. I remember that when I first went to eat at a restaurant in Fort Worth where candles were lit on the table for atmosphere, I almost broke down and cried. Candles here are decoration, but in my old country, they were often our only source of light.

The waves of gratitude that wash over me are overwhelming and very emotional at times. During one spring break trip we visited Washington, DC. Don was excited for me to see our nation's capital, but I don't think he was prepared for my reaction to each special place we visited.

One of those moments was at the White House. We arrived early on a beautiful spring morning, and I was wide-eyed and quivering. I grabbed Don's hand because I couldn't speak. I had to stand there and collect myself before we actually joined the tour.

"What is it?" Don asked, knowing that I was overcome somehow. He was concerned, but I think he suspected what was happening. "Are you okay? Do you need to just hang out a minute?"

I looked around at the soaring ceilings inside this grand building, blinking back tears. I took a couple of deep breaths and finally found my voice.

"It's just so incredible to me that we can come to the American capital and we can just walk into these phenomenal buildings. Nobody asks us for documents. Nobody challenges us or says we don't have the right to walk into this beautiful place." In Vietnam, unless you work there, walking into a government building is absolutely unheard of. That moment walking through the White House, a place that represents the past, present, and future of this country, lodged deep in my heart, and I loved my new home more than ever.

I'm stunned at how much we take for granted in our world here. We can travel anywhere, see anything. And even in my workday world, I am reminded how fortunate we are to do as we wish. Here in America, we are surrounded by endless possibilities for taking care of ourselves and for looking as good as we like. I have clients who are seventy years old, and they look fabulous because they have the right tools to take care of themselves. You can't do that where I come from.

People have said that they see me as being someone who works too hard, but my life would be missing something if I didn't spend time with these incredible people I know through my work. And don't forget, helping people look beautiful has always been close to my heart. It makes me happy because I remember how hard it was when I was little, when I would have given anything to have pretty hair and the "right" skin color. My goal is always to make people feel good because they're happy with themselves and the way they look.

And, yes, it goes without saying that working in a salon means I'm in the position of hearing clients who want to overshare. But early on, my clients understood that I don't want to gossip. I'm grateful for the opportunities I have and would never want to betray the generous people who helped me create this career. I'd rather know what makes people happy. Blessed with many gracious customers who have helped me improve my English and who mentor me on American culture, I'm so grateful for the genuine friendships that have developed through my work. Having these wonderful people treat someone like me with love and respect brings me a joy and warmth that is hard to contain, and I hope I will be able to return these gifts to them in equal measure before I leave this earth.

In the midst of all these blessings, I continue to hear about and see young people born to wonderful lives who take it all for granted. Just as often, I read about and see young people resentful that the world has not been handed to them. I want to yell from the rooftops, "You have opportunity to get and do and be whatever you want. You need to be willing to work hard for it!" If I could show these people a grim snapshot of the life that exists in Vietnam, where people want to work hard but don't have the opportunity, I would. In plenty of places around the world, you don't get to just show up for a job interview, get hired for your abilities, and then work for success. That sort of fairness does not happen in many places on this planet of ours. Here, by comparison, it is simple: play by the rules, work hard, and all kinds of good things can happen. I am living proof.

This frustration and fear hits very close to home for me. My daughter Sydney sees my clients with their fabulous homes, and some even with guards at their gates, and she says, "Oh, I want to grow up and be that rich," as if wealth is something expected or easy. And I answer her, "Do you know how to get that kind of life? Your opportunity is in front of you. You're in a great school, so you must work hard now, get a good education, and get a good job if you plan to make a lot of money and get the life you want. Don't expect someone to just give it to you."

I explain to her that the school she goes to has a lot of wealthy kids, and I explain that we don't have that kind of money. Although she may not get the same clothing or cars, I want her to realize that what makes you important is what's in your brain and in your character. I keep telling her she needs to concentrate on education and not worry about money. I really believe that if you have the right head and right heart, everything else will come.

The caution I want Sydney to understand is this: if she grows up focused on finding a rich husband, she needs to understand that accomplishing that does not guarantee happiness. I've seen some wealthy people who are miserable because somehow the values they needed got misplaced. And I know some women who can't balance a checkbook or take care of themselves financially, and I have seen some of them suffer horribly as a result.

Witnessing the collapse of those women's lives has led me to be even more focused on making sure my children know how to manage money and take care of business.

Naturally, growing up in such a poor country shaped my philosophies. I'm glad that when I arrived in the United States, my goals were basic—I wouldn't let the fact that I was starting with absolutely nothing slow me down. You cannot be ashamed that you don't have what someone else has. You cannot spend time being jealous of what others have. You search out your opportunities and are grateful when you find them.

Since living here and creating this life for myself, I am certain that getting bills paid and living within your means is the road to independence. The best advice I can give to kids Scott's age is to learn to handle money well. Avoid the big student loans that so many take on without much thought for the future, and don't sign up for credit cards that tempt you into debt. In other words, avoid the insanity of the must-have-it-now mentality, and you can enjoy the best part of life in America—freedom.

Some might say that my focus on saving money and living as practically as humanly possible has its downside. I have to admit, it's still hard for me to let my hair down and just have fun—if that means spending a dime. Even though we have money in the bank and our home and cars are paid for, I'm still very cautious. When Scott or Sydney asks me for something, even if it costs no more than five dollars, my immediate response is "No!" Eventually, of course, they've figured out to ask Don for things.

Don, thank God, is a good balance for me. I like to say that he's a kid in a candy store: although he's smart with money, he enjoys spending it in a way that I sometimes think is crazy. When he wants to buy me jewelry, I say, "Don't you dare!" When he was sending me flowers all the time, I finally told him to go to the store, put them in a vase and bring them to me to save on the delivery charge! But Don has helped me learn to enjoy the life we've built. He says we've worked hard, and we need to start to balance our life before it is too late. He even understands what's going on inside of me when I come home from work and start cleaning the house just to relieve the stress I'm feeling. Early on, Don would help me because he hates to see me working by myself. But over the years, he's realized that he doesn't want to stay up until 1:00 a.m. cleaning—sometimes even on New Year's Eve. He's also realized that when I go on one of these cleaning binges, I need to be reminded that I've earned my moments of rest.

While Don has helped me learn to relax, my strengthening faith has also helped me learn to be more confident and less intense. God has taught me that as long as our priorities are correct, we will always have what we truly need. Certainly it's helped me overcome the challenges of building this new life here. Without a doubt, my belief in God gives me strength and has gotten me through my struggles with my mother and all the fears that plagued me while I was looking after her and raising Scott alone. And perhaps most of all, my certainty that God will guide me through any trouble is what has lifted me above that sense of despair and lost hope that filled my childhood.

It might seem strange that I end this memoir retelling a story from the beginning of my life, but perhaps that's how we live, always circling back in our memories to those places that first made us what we are. It is the memory of the flood, the one that almost took my life when I was fourteen.

That midday break on a school day, I was digging in the garden, one of the chores my mother had assigned me. It had been raining hard for days, and most of my neighbors feared a flood. While I was working on my hands and knees in the mud, the rain fell in thicker and thicker sheets, until people all around me on the nearby roads and in the fields shouted warnings.

"Run! Run! It's flooding!" was the only thing I could make out clearly. I began to run, my heart thudding in my chest, fear gripping my throat. My legs moved as fast as I could make them. I could barely see where I was going in the blinding rain, but through the confusion and fear, a voice whispered in my head, *"Troi con thuong con."* The words I heard meant, "God still loves me."

No one in the fields or roads that day had any business trying to run or walk home during the rain. We needed boats. In a panic, I realized I was lost because the water had covered the well-worn path that always took me home. Just as I was about to be carried away in the torrent of water, I made out some familiar trees and other landmarks just a few feet ahead of me. There it was! That was where the pathway to my house should have been, if it hadn't been swallowed by the flood.

Suddenly, the rain stopped. The river of water immediately subsided. I could step onto the path and follow it home. Just as I reached my house and stepped inside, the heavy rain began again and the flooding resumed—but I was safe. I knew this was a miracle, a God thing. And I began to realize it's all about God's plan, not mine.

While I began to understand that God was looking out for me, we didn't live in a place—a part of Vietnam held tight in the grip of communism—where saying such things aloud was tolerated. For years, I kept my thoughts to myself. It wasn't until we prepared for our move to the United States that I found myself in a situation where a person could discuss his or her faith openly.

Once we were in Saigon, gathering information about the new life we would soon be living, I learned that the freedom to go to church awaited us. When we reached the Philippines, I hadn't forgotten my experience in the flood, and I began going to church right away, though I didn't really understand a lot about the Bible because it was in English. Eventually I came to understand that God doesn't want a lot—he just wants our hearts

Sau outside her salon. *Photo by Robin Sanders.*

Sau with Jean Roach at the salon. *Photo by Michael Toole.*

Sau coloring Robin Sanders's hair. *Photo by Patty Thompson.*

Sau on the phone at her salon. *Photo by Dee Dee Flores.*

Sau and Sydney spending time with America's first First Family in the Ford Orientation Center at Mount Vernon. *Photo by Don Hudecek.*

and our trust and our faith.

After I came to Fort Worth, I met clients who had the time to go to Bible study, and discussions with them fueled my interest in exploring my faith further. Now with Don, we go to church and Bible study, and I'm getting more familiar with a book that was so long forbidden to me. Don is incredibly patient as he helps me catch up with the readings, and I've come a long way.

Halfway through the writing of this book, I finally opened my own salon. I had sacrificed, I had prepared, but ultimately, it was God who placed it in my path. When my previous salon was closing, I prayed for a new place to call my work home, a place where I would stay until I retire. Since I never believed that I could buy an *actual* salon, I kept looking at old houses to turn into my new workplace. And then a salon popped up— for sale—with its customer base intact. There was only one explanation for my good fortune—God gave me what I needed, actually more than I need, something bigger than I thought possible. For me, this moment was about becoming whole.

Finally, blessedly, with the help of Don, my children, my incredible friends, and my faith, I realize that although the difficulty and adversity I have experienced were deeply painful, they are a part of who I am. I sacrificed pieces of my life to pick myself up, feed my family, and accomplish my goals. I missed Scott's soccer games, Sydney's parent luncheons, and weekend family time. These were difficult decisions. Some were good, and looking back, some were not so good, but sacrifice was necessary to give everyone a better future. I could have cried and allowed myself to be overwhelmed and curl up and die, or do what my ex-husband did, which was to drown himself in drink and abandon our son, but I didn't. Instead, I stood up and buckled up, took stock of what we had, thanked God for it, and then did what needed to be done to get to the next step. One step at a time. Always grateful for the last and current step, but always aiming higher.

All of these memories had a role in making me the strong woman and grateful survivor that I am today. What happened to that heartbroken child who lost a sister and endured such shame delivered by the legacies of war? Through the miracle of grace, that very girl grew into a woman firmly gripping the enduring, indestructible lifeline of hope.

Postscript

Why did I want to write this book?

I wanted my children to know and be reminded how blessed they are to know God and to live in America, allowing them to enjoy the freedoms and opportunities it makes available to us, and not take these for granted.

I wanted to thank God because without his protection I wouldn't be alive today. Looking back I can identify where he has protected me ever since that day of the flood in Vietnam where I acknowledged Him. I thank God for giving me the glimmer of hope to keep going and to keep a positive mind-set, and for putting angels in my path. Even though someone may feel that the world is too big for them and believe they have no hope, God loves us all, and he is the source of hope that will give you the strength to pick yourself up and move on from where you are to a better place.

I have so many things to thank America for—even for things as basic as clean, running water and safe food. Most importantly I thank America for the opportunities and freedoms it offers, and I thank the people who sacrificed to gain and maintain these freedoms. I want my children to know that we have been handed a gift and that we are its stewards who must keep it alive for the next generation.

I worked hard to reach my goals, but working hard gets you nowhere if you are not allowed to benefit from the fruits of your labor.

About the Author

Photo by Erin Potter

Sau Le Hudecek arrived in the United States in 1993, at the age of 22, and was sworn in as a citizen in 2001. She owns a successful salon in Fort Worth, Texas, where she continues to support her own elite clientele. She lives with her family in Granbury, where she enjoys the sunsets from their home on the lake.